CRAZY
IS THE NEW
NORMAL

**COVER ART BY
TOM TOMORROW**

**COLLECTION EDITS BY
JUSTIN EISINGER**

**PUBLISHER
TED ADAMS**

Become our fan on Facebook **facebook.com/idwpublishing**
Follow us on Twitter **@idwpublishing**
Subscribe to us on YouTube **youtube.com/idwpublishing**
See what's new on Tumblr **tumblr.idwpublishing.com**
Check us out on Instagram **instagram.com/idwpublishing**

ISBN: 978-1-63140-700-0   19 18 17 16   1 2 3 4

Originally published weekly as THIS MODERN WORLD.

Ted Adams, CEO & Publisher
Greg Goldstein, President & COO
Robbie Robbins, EVP/Sr. Graphic Artist
Chris Ryall, Chief Creative Officer/Editor-in-Chief
Matthew Ruzicka, CPA, Chief Financial Officer
Dirk Wood, VP of Marketing
Lorelei Bunjes, VP of Digital Services
Jeff Webber, VP of Digital Publishing & Business Development
Jerry Bennington, VP of New Product Development

For international rights, please contact
licensing@idwpublishing.com

CRAZY IS THE NEW NORMAL

by tom tomorrow

also by tom tomorrow

Greetings From This Modern World
Tune in Tomorrow
The Wrath of Sparky
When Penguins Attack
Penguin Soup for the Soul
The Great Big Book of Tomorrow
Hell in a Handbasket
The Future's So Bright, I Can't Bear to Look
The Very Silly Mayor
Too Much Crazy
The World of Tomorrow
25 Years of Tomorrow

For my father

THIS MODERN WORLD

by TOM TOMORROW

Ask Mister Republican Man!

I'M HERE TO **HELP!**

Dear Mister Republican Man: My boss is constantly berating me! How can I stand up for myself without getting fired? --Hassled in Hartford

I'D SUGGEST YOU PUT YOUR PETTY WORKPLACE GRIEVANCES **ASIDE** AND FOCUS ON WHAT **REALLY** MATTERS-- THE **BENGHAZI SCANDAL!**

IT'S WORSE THAN **WATERGATE,** YOU KNOW!

Dear Mister Republican Man: My friend won't stop talking about her new boyfriend, and it's driving me nuts! -- Exasperated in Englewood

IS YOUR FRIEND A **DEMOCRAT?** SHE **COULD** BE TRYING TO DIS-TRACT YOU -- FROM **BENGHAZI!**

MAYBE YOU NEED A **NEW** FRIEND.

Dear Mister Republican Man: my husband is acting distant and stay-ing late at the office most evenings. Do you think he's having an affair? --Distraught in Des Moines

I THINK IT'S **MORE** LIKELY THAT HE'S PREOCCUPIED BY THE OBAMA ADMINISTRATION'S COVER-UP OF **BENGHAZI!**

AS YOU SHOULD BE AS WELL.

Dear Mister Republican Man: my teenager spends all his free time on the internet! Should I be worried? --Apprehensive in Allentown

I SEE NOTHING TO WORRY ABOUT-- AS LONG AS HE'S READING UP ON **BENGHAZI!**

SUCH CURIOSITY IS **ENTIRELY NATURAL** AT HIS AGE!

Dear Mister Republican Man: I'm OBSESSED with Benghazi! My wife left me, I lost my job, and I'm about to be evicted! What should I DO?? --Fixated in Fargo

WHY DO **ANYTHING?** YOU SOUND **PERFECTLY** WELL-ADJUSTED TO **ME!**

IF ONLY WE HAD **MORE** LIKE YOU!

NEXT Dear Mr. Re-publican Man-- **BENGHAZI!** THE ANSWER IS ALWAYS **BENGHAZI!**

TOM TOMORROW ©2014

1

THIS MODERN WORLD

by TOM TOMORROW

*ACTUAL QUOTE FROM 1/3/14 COLUMN!

2

THIS MODERN WORLD

by TOM TOMORROW

THIS MODERN WORLD

by TOM TOMORROW

Panel 1: IF THE WATER SUPPLY FOR 300,000 PEOPLE WERE POISONED BY *TERRORISTS*, IT WOULD BE A NATIONAL EMERGENCY.

WE WILL ADDRESS THIS CRISIS WITH EVERY RESOURCE AT OUR *DISPOSAL*! THE PURITY OF HOMELAND DRINKING WATER WILL BE PROTECTED AT *ANY COST*!

NOW PLEASE STAY INSIDE AND DUCT TAPE YOUR FAUCETS UNTIL FURTHER NOTICE.

Panel 2: FRIGHTENED AMERICANS WOULD EMBRACE WHATEVER NEW SECURITY MEASURES WERE RUSHED INTO LAW.

ANYONE CAUGHT HIKING NEAR A *RESERVOIR* OR PICNICKING ON A *RIVERBANK* WILL BE SUBJECT TO *IMMEDIATE ARREST*!

I NEVER TRUSTED THOSE TYPES ANYWAY!

Panel 3: A LOT OF VERY SERIOUS THINKERS WOULD INSIST THAT WE NEEDED TO BOMB SOMEBODY.

HOW ABOUT *IRAN*? THEY'D BE A GOOD TARGET!

SURE, THERE'S NO EVIDENCE LINKING THEM TO THE ATTACK--

--BUT WHO *CARES*? WE JUST NEED TO MAKE A *STATEMENT*!

Panel 4: THE ASSAULT ON CIVIL LIBERTIES WOULD SHIFT INTO OVEDRDRIVE.

THE NSA MUST SCOOP UP EVEN *MORE* METADATA--IN ORDER TO KEEP YOU SAFE *NEXT* TIME!

MAYBE.

ALSO WE SHOULD DRONE SNOWDEN, JUST BECAUSE.

Panel 5: AND OF COURSE CABLE NEWS WOULD BE ON THE TOPIC 24/7.

SO YOU SEE, WATER IS *TWO* PARTS HYDROGEN AND *ONE* PART OXYGEN!

FASCINATING! AND WOULD YOU SAY IT'S ESSENTIAL TO LIFE AS WE *KNOW* IT?

NO QUESTION! WATER IS *VERY, VERY* IMPORTANT!

THERE YOU HAVE IT--THE *SCIENTIFIC* PERSPECTIVE!

Panel 6: BUT SINCE A *CORPORATION* DID IT, NO BIG DEAL.

EH, STUFF HAPPENS. WHAT CAN YOU DO.

NO POINT IN CRYING OVER SPILLED 4-METHYL-CYCLOHEXANE METHANOL, THAT'S WHAT *I* ALWAYS SAY!

TOM TOMORROW ©2014

THIS MODERN WORLD

by TOM TOMORROW

Panel 1

FLUFFY BUNNY AND HAPPY MOUSE IN "*SUPPORT THE DRONES!*"

I'M *CONFUSED*, HAPPY MOUSE! YOU KNOW HOW SUPPORTERS OF DRONE WARFARE ALWAYS SAY THAT DRONES PROTECT THE LIVES OF AMERICAN *SOLDIERS*?

UH HUH..?

Panel 2

WELL, ACCORDING TO THE NEW YORK TIMES, THE ADMINISTRATION WANTS TO KEEP EIGHT TO TWELVE THOUSAND TROOPS IN AFGHANISTAN *AFTER* THE OFFICIAL END OF THE WAR--

Panel 3

--AND ONE OF THE OPENLY ACKNOWLEDGED REASONS FOR DOING SO IS THAT THE C.I.A. DOESN'T WANT TO LOSE CONTROL OF ITS *DRONE BASES!*

Panel 4

SO IN OTHER WORDS, INSTEAD OF DRONES SUPPOSEDLY PROTECTING THE TROOPS--

--WE'D BE LEAVING TROOPS IN HARM'S WAY--TO PROTECT THE *DRONES!*

IT JUST SEEMS--

Panel 5

AHEM.

ULP!

UH--

Panel 6

--IT SEEMS LIKE AN *ENTIRELY REASONABLE STRATEGY* THAT I CAN'T IMAGINE *ANYONE* OBJECTING TO!

U.S.A! U.S.A!

THAT'S WHAT I *THOUGHT* YOU WERE GOING TO SAY!

GOSH, FLUFFY BUNNY, THAT ROBOT DEATH PLANE--

--CAN STILL HEAR YOU!

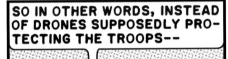

TOM TOMORROW ©2014

5

THIS MODERN WORLD

by TOM TOMORROW

News item: half of American sports fans think God intervenes in sporting events.

I CANNOT **BELIEVE** THE BRONCOS DUMPED MY GOOD AND FAITHFUL SERVANT, TIM TEBOW!

I SHALL EXACT **RETRIBUTION**--AND SEND UNTO THEM A **HUMILIATING** SUPER BOWL DEFEAT!

HALLOWED BE THY NAME, SIR.

SUFFER MY FEARSOME **WRATH**, INSOLENT FOOTBALL FRANCHISE!

SO, UH, GOD, SIR--ABOUT ALL THOSE FORMER PLAYERS WITH **BRAIN INJURIES**--?

DO YOU **MIND**? I'M TRYING TO WATCH THE **GAME** HERE!

GO SEA-HAWKS!

Panel 1: OVER THE YEARS, INCOME INEQUALITY CONTINUED TO RISE...UNTIL FINALLY, *ONE RICH GUY* OWNED AS MUCH AS THE REST OF THE PLANET *COMBINED.*

Forbes

THE ONE RICH GUY
HE OWNS EVERYTHING

Panel 2: WITH SO MUCH WEALTH IN ONE GUY'S HANDS, EVERYONE ELSE HAD TO TIGHTEN THEIR BELTS AND MAKE DO WITH A LITTLE *LESS.*

I REMEMBER WHEN WE HAD SCHOOLS AND POLICE AND FIRE DEPARTMENTS! WHY THERE WERE *STREET LIGHTS* OUT IN FRONT OF YOUR *HOUSE* AT NIGHT!

WHAT'S A "HOUSE"?

Panel 3: OCCASIONALLY SOMEONE MADE A MILDLY CRITICAL REMARK ABOUT THE ONE RICH GUY--

@StarvingPeon: He sure owns a lot of the planet's resources!

HOW *DARE* THEY! THIS IS WORSE THAN HITLER, STALIN AND VLAD THE IMPALER *COMBINED!*

TRACK THIS PERSON DOWN AND HAVE THEM KILLED.

YES SIR.

Panel 4: --BUT THE PURVEYORS OF CONVENTIONAL WISDOM WERE ALWAYS QUICK TO DEFEND HIM AS A *JOB CREATOR.*

IF YOU CAN'T GET A JOB BUILDING HIS GIANT HOVER-YACHTS OR SCRUBBING HIS SOLID GOLD TOILETS--

--*ON* HIS GIANT HOVER-YACHTS--

--YOU MUST NOT *WANT* TO WORK!

Sunday Talking About Stuff SHOW

Panel 5: SINCE THE ONE RICH GUY WAS THE ONLY REMAINING SOURCE OF CAMPAIGN CONTRIBUTIONS, FEW POLITICIANS DARED TO CROSS HIM.

IF WE RAISED HIS TAXES *EVER* SO SLIGHTLY--PERHAPS WE COULD REPAIR *SOME* OF OUR REMAINING INFRASTRUCTURE...?

WHY DO YOU WANT TO PUNISH HIS SUCCESS?

YOU BIG GOVERNMENT SPENDOCRATS MAKE ME *SICK!*

Panel 6: EVENTUALLY, AMERICANS GREW ANGRY AT THE SHEER INJUSTICE OF IT ALL AND ROSE UP IN *REVOLUTION*--NAH, JUST KIDDING.

I'M NOT THE ONE RICH GUY *NOW*--BUT MAYBE SOMEDAY I *WILL* BE! AND I SURE DON'T WANT TO HAVE TO PAY HIGH TAXES *THEN!*

BESIDES, CAPITALISM WILL *ALWAYS* HAVE LOSERS AND WINNERS.

WELL, A WINNER.

RIGHT.

...AND THE ONE RICH GUY LIVED *HAPPILY EVER AFTER!*

TOM TOMORROW ©2014

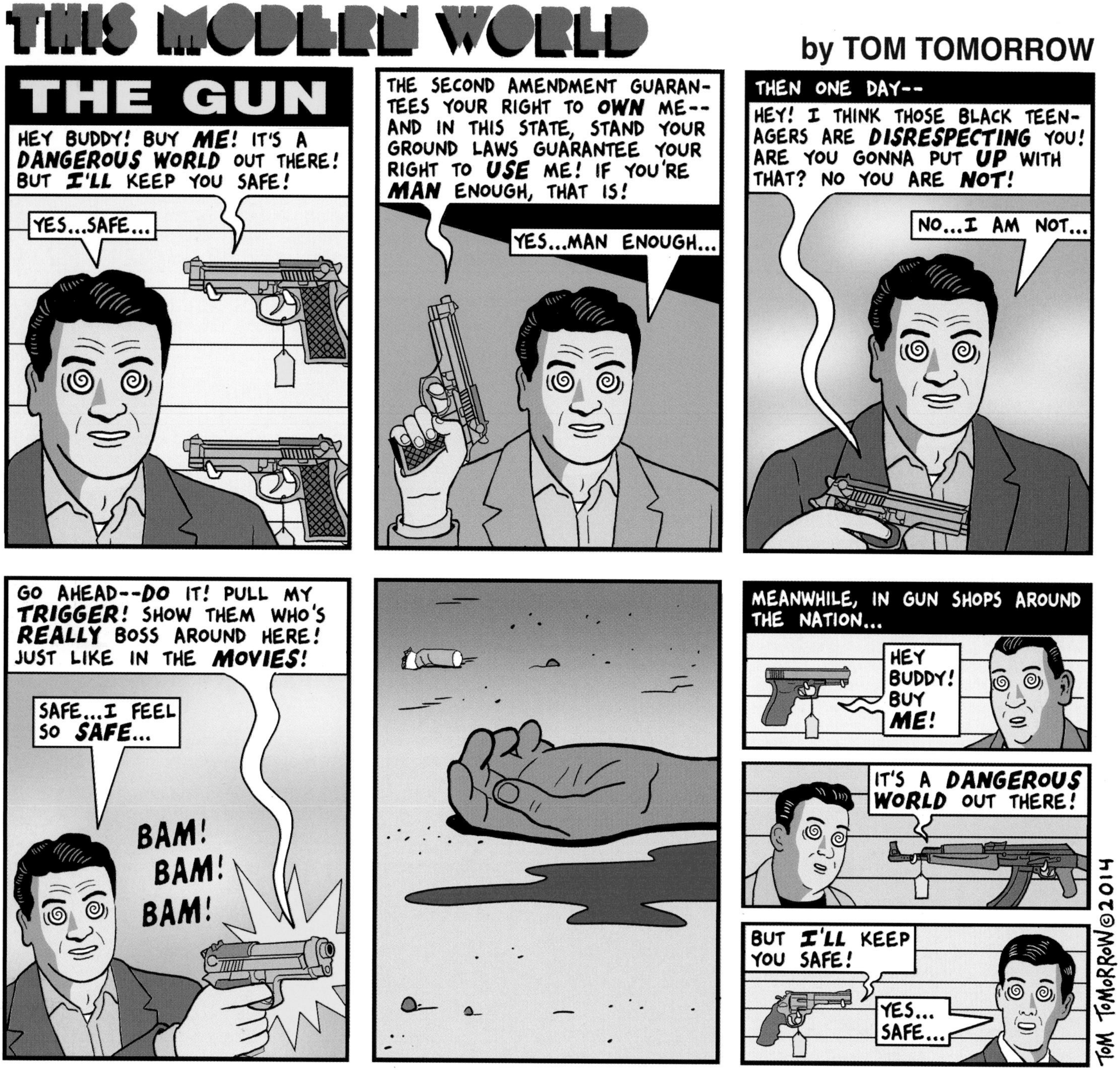
THIS MODERN WORLD
by TOM TOMORROW
THE GUN
HEY BUDDY! BUY ME! IT'S A DANGEROUS WORLD OUT THERE! BUT I'LL KEEP YOU SAFE!
YES...SAFE...
THE SECOND AMENDMENT GUARANTEES YOUR RIGHT TO OWN ME-- AND IN THIS STATE, STAND YOUR GROUND LAWS GUARANTEE YOUR RIGHT TO USE ME! IF YOU'RE MAN ENOUGH, THAT IS!
YES...MAN ENOUGH...
THEN ONE DAY--
HEY! I THINK THOSE BLACK TEENAGERS ARE DISRESPECTING YOU! ARE YOU GONNA PUT UP WITH THAT? NO YOU ARE NOT!
NO...I AM NOT...
GO AHEAD--DO IT! PULL MY TRIGGER! SHOW THEM WHO'S REALLY BOSS AROUND HERE! JUST LIKE IN THE MOVIES!
SAFE...I FEEL SO SAFE...
BAM!
BAM!
BAM!
MEANWHILE, IN GUN SHOPS AROUND THE NATION...
HEY BUDDY! BUY ME!
IT'S A DANGEROUS WORLD OUT THERE!
BUT I'LL KEEP YOU SAFE!
YES... SAFE...
TOM TOMORROW©2014

THIS MODERN WORLD

by TOM TOMORROW

Panel 1: WE TRY TO PRESENT A FACADE OF RATIONALITY TO THE WORLD--

I CHANGE THE BATTERIES IN MY SMOKE ALARMS ONCE A YEAR!

I FLOSS AFTER *EVERY* MEAL!

I MAKE BACKUPS OF MY *BACKUPS*!

Panel 2: --BUT THERE'S ALWAYS A CAULDRON OF CRAZY SIMMERING JUST BENEATH THE SURFACE.

IF I DON'T WEAR MY LUCKY UNDERPANTS MY TEAM WILL SURELY *LOSE!*

LIBERALS INVENTED GLOBAL WARMING BECAUSE THEY *HATE FREEDOM.*

I'VE TOTALLY GOT A SHOT WITH GWYNETH.

Panel 3: CONSIDER THE HOBBY LOBBY CASE.

I BELIEVE IN AN INVISIBLE, OMNISCIENT SKY BEING WHO *VEHEMENTLY* OPPOSES INSURANCE COVERAGE FOR CERTAIN KINDS OF BIRTH CONTROL.

MAKES PERFECT SENSE TO *ME!*

Panel 4: NOT ONLY ARE THE CHAIN'S OWNERS TAKEN *SERIOUSLY*--THEY MAY EVEN SUCCEED IN CHANGING THE *LAW*.

WE MUST *RESPECT* THEIR SINCERELY-HELD CONVICTION THAT GOD DISAPPROVES OF THE EMPLOYER MANDATE THEY DON'T LIKE.

THOUGH THE BIBLE *IS* ADMITTEDLY AMBIGUOUS ON THE QUESTION OF INSURANCE COVERAGE.

Panel 5: *OR*--CONSIDER THE CREATIONISTS WHO THINK *THEY* SHOULD GET EQUAL TIME ON NEIL DEGRASSE TYSON'S NEW "COSMOS" SERIES.

ON THE ONE HAND YOU'VE GOT SCIENTIFIC CONSENSUS AND OBSERVABLE PHENOMENA--

--AND ON THE OTHER, *BIBLE STORIES!*

PRETTY MUCH THE SAME THING!

Panel 6: AND SPEAKING OF *IRRATIONALITY*...

SO DID THE MISSING PLANE FLY INTO A *BLACK HOLE*? DID A *GREMLIN* RIP OFF ITS WINGS LIKE IN THAT OLD "TWILIGHT ZONE" EPISODE?

AND *WHY* WON'T THE AUTHORITIES CONSULT WITH A *REPUTABLE PSYCHIC*--TO FIND OUT THE *TRUTH*?!

THE MYSTERIOUS MYSTERY OF FLIGHT 370

WHERE IS IT? WHERE IS IT? WHERE IS IT?

BREAKING NEWS: PLANE STILL MISSING

MUCH MYSTERY • SO CONFUSE • WOW

TOM TOMORROW ©2014

9

THIS MODERN WORLD

by TOM TOMORROW

SUNDAY TALKING ABOUT STUFF SHOW

--AND FOR MORE INSIGHT INTO THE WORST CRISIS OBAMA HAS FACED SINCE THE LAST CRISIS, WE TURN NOW TO THE *BELLIGERENT NEOCON!*

LINDSEY GRAHAM HAD IT *EXACTLY RIGHT!*

PUTIN WOULD HAVE *NEVER* INVADED UKRAINE--IF NOT FOR THE WEAKNESS OBAMA DEMONSTRATED IN *BENGHAZI!*

NOT TO MENTION THE BUNGLED OBAMACARE ROLLOUT.

AND THE IRS SCANDAL.

AND THOSE MOM JEANS HE WEARS!

FASCINATING! BUT WHAT SHOULD OBAMA DO *NOW?*

OBVIOUSLY HE MUST TAKE *DECISIVE ACTION!* INVOLVING *LEADERSHIP!* AND *STRENGTH!* AND STUFF.

I *SEE!*

INEFFECTUAL MODERATE-- WHAT SAY *YOU?*

I *TOO* BELIEVE WE MUST TAKE ACTION--BUT OUR OPTIONS *ARE* LIMITED--

WHAT ARE YOU--SOME KIND OF *APPEASENIK?*

WE ARE *ALL* UKRAINIANS *NOW!*

I--WHAT?

HASHTAG PUTIN *SUCKS!*

WELL THERE'S *ONE* THING WE CAN ALL AGREE ON--COUNTRIES WHICH INVADE SMALLER COUNTRIES ON A PRETEXT HAVE *NO* MORAL AUTHORITY!

THAT'S FOR SURE!

CAN YOU EVEN *IMAGINE?*

♪

COUGH

OKAY THEN! COMING UP NEXT: COULD OBAMA DEFEAT PUTIN MANO-A-MANO IN A *BARE-KNUCKLE BOXING MATCH?*

WE'LL SEE WHAT THE BELLIGERENT NEOCON THINKS!

FIRST THESE MESSAGES.

TOM TOMORROW ©2014

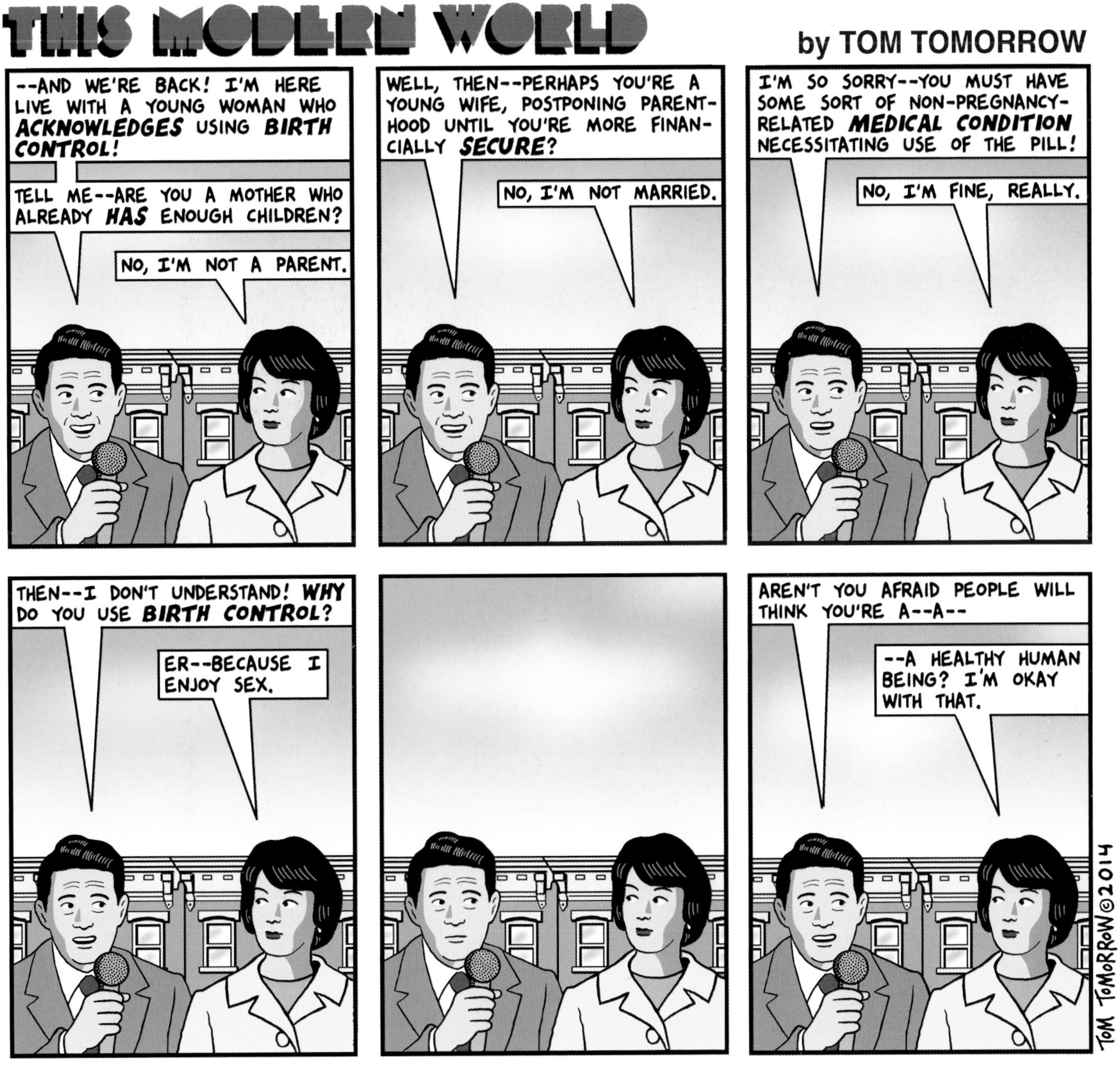
THIS MODERN WORLD
by TOM TOMORROW
--AND WE'RE BACK! I'M HERE LIVE WITH A YOUNG WOMAN WHO ACKNOWLEDGES USING BIRTH CONTROL!
TELL ME--ARE YOU A MOTHER WHO ALREADY HAS ENOUGH CHILDREN?
NO, I'M NOT A PARENT.
WELL, THEN--PERHAPS YOU'RE A YOUNG WIFE, POSTPONING PARENTHOOD UNTIL YOU'RE MORE FINANCIALLY SECURE?
NO, I'M NOT MARRIED.
I'M SO SORRY--YOU MUST HAVE SOME SORT OF NON-PREGNANCY-RELATED MEDICAL CONDITION NECESSITATING USE OF THE PILL!
NO, I'M FINE, REALLY.
THEN--I DON'T UNDERSTAND! WHY DO YOU USE BIRTH CONTROL?
ER--BECAUSE I ENJOY SEX.
AREN'T YOU AFRAID PEOPLE WILL THINK YOU'RE A--A--
--A HEALTHY HUMAN BEING? I'M OKAY WITH THAT.
TOM TOMORROW©2014

THIS MODERN WORLD

by TOM TOMORROW

Panel 1: THE REVELATIONS KEPT LEAKING OUT.

WE ONLY TRACK *METADATA*!

ER, AND *SOME* CONTENT.

OKAY, *ALL* CONTENT-- BUT JUST FROM *SOME* COUNTRIES.

ER--

Panel 2: EVENTUALLY IT TURNED OUT THE N.S.A. WAS RECORDING EVERYTHING, EVERYWHERE.

OKAY, FINE--IF IT HAPPENED NEAR A PHONE OR A WEBCAM, WE'VE GOT A RECORD OF IT.

WE CALL IT TOTALLY *AWESOME* INFORMATION AWARENESS.

Panel 3: AS USUAL, AMERICANS TOOK THE NEWS IN STRIDE.

IT SAYS HERE THEY'VE GOT A MASSIVE VIDEO ARCHIVE OF EVERY- THING EVERYONE HAS SAID OR DONE IN PUBLIC *OR* PRIVATE FOR THE PAST FIVE YEARS!

AH, THAT'S *OLD NEWS*!

EVERYBODY ALREADY *KNEW* THEY WERE DOING *THAT*!

Panel 4: CONGRESS DIDN'T *END* THE SUR- VEILLANCE, OF COURSE--BUT THEY *DID* STREAMLINE THE *FOIA* PROCESS...

YOUR REQUEST FOR INFORMATION HAS BEEN APPROVED! ACCORDING TO OUR RECORDS, YOUR KEYS ARE IN THE BEIGE JACKET YOU THREW ON THE LARGE EASY CHAIR IN THE *LIVING ROOM* LAST NIGHT!

GREAT! THANKS!

Panel 5: ...AND EVENTUALLY, PEOPLE MOSTLY AGREED THAT PRIVACY HAD ALWAYS BEEN OVERRATED ANYWAY.

YOUR WIFE IS CORRECT, SIR--AT TIMESTAMP 20:23:43, YOU DO IN FACT RESPOND TO HER IN A "SNIPPY" TONE OF VOICE!

OH! MY MIS- TAKE, THEN!

20:19:52

20:23:43

Panel 6: BUT *THEN*--

IT SAYS HERE THE N.S.A. HAS BEEN SECRETLY HARVESTING OUR BRAINS WITH NANOBOTS AND DOWNLOADING OUR VERY *THOUGHTS* AND *MEMO- RIES* INTO THEIR SERVERS!

AH, THAT'S *OLD NEWS*!

EVERYBODY ALREADY *KNEW* THEY WERE DOING *THAT*!

Panel 7: AND THEN--

HELLO, N.S.A? I JUST LOST MY TRAIN OF THOUGHT!

ONE MOMENT-- I'LL LOOK IT UP FOR YOU.

TOM TOMORROW ©2014

THIS MODERN WORLD

by TOM TOMORROW

WE TRY TO PRESENT A FACADE OF RATIONALITY TO THE WORLD--

I CHANGE THE BATTERIES IN MY SMOKE ALARMS ONCE A YEAR!

I FLOSS AFTER *EVERY* MEAL!

I MAKE BACKUPS OF MY *BACKUPS!*

--BUT THERE'S ALWAYS A CAULDRON OF CRAZY SIMMERING JUST BENEATH THE SURFACE.

IF I DON'T WEAR MY LUCKY UNDERPANTS MY TEAM WILL SURELY *LOSE!*

LIBERALS INVENTED GLOBAL WARMING BECAUSE THEY *HATE FREEDOM.*

I'VE TOTALLY GOT A SHOT WITH GWYNETH.

CONSIDER THE HOBBY LOBBY CASE.

I BELIEVE IN AN INVISIBLE, OMNISCIENT SKY BEING WHO *VEHEMENTLY* OPPOSES INSURANCE COVERAGE FOR CERTAIN KINDS OF BIRTH CONTROL.

MAKES PERFECT SENSE TO *ME!*

HOBBY LOBBY

NOT ONLY ARE THE CHAIN'S OWNERS TAKEN *SERIOUSLY*--THEY MAY EVEN SUCCEED IN CHANGING THE *LAW.*

WE MUST *RESPECT* THEIR SINCERELY-HELD CONVICTION THAT GOD DISAPPROVES OF THE EMPLOYER MANDATE THEY DON'T LIKE.

THOUGH THE BIBLE *IS* ADMITTEDLY AMBIGUOUS ON THE QUESTION OF INSURANCE COVERAGE.

OR--CONSIDER THE CREATIONISTS WHO THINK *THEY* SHOULD GET EQUAL TIME ON NEIL DEGRASSE TYSON'S NEW "*COSMOS*" SERIES.

ON THE ONE HAND YOU'VE GOT SCIENTIFIC CONSENSUS AND OBSERVABLE PHENOMENA--

--AND ON THE OTHER, *BIBLE STORIES!*

PRETTY MUCH THE SAME THING!

AND SPEAKING OF *IRRATIONALITY...*

SO DID THE MISSING PLANE FLY INTO A *BLACK HOLE?* DID A *GREMLIN* RIP OFF ITS WINGS LIKE IN THAT OLD "*TWILIGHT ZONE*" EPISODE?

AND *WHY* WON'T THE AUTHORITIES CONSULT WITH A *REPUTABLE PSYCHIC*--TO FIND OUT THE *TRUTH?!*

THE MYSTERIOUS MYSTERY OF FLIGHT 370

WHERE IS IT? WHERE IS IT? WHERE IS IT?

BREAKING NEWS: PLANE STILL MISSING

MUCH MYSTERY • SO CONFUSE • WOW

TOM TOMORROW ©2014

THIS MODERN WORLD

by TOM TOMORROW

SCIENCE STUFF
— with your host —
THE RIGHT WING SCIENCE DUDE

TODAY WE'LL LOOK AT GLOBAL WARMING--MALICIOUS **HOAX** OR PERNICIOUS **LIE**?

SKEPTICAL FREETHINKERS JUST WANT TO HAVE A **DEBATE**!

FUNDED BY OUR FRIENDS THE KOCH BROTHERS.

FOLKS, TAKE IT FROM A GUY IN A LAB COAT--WE DON'T NEED TO WASTE ANY MORE OF OUR NATION'S VALUABLE **SCIENCE TIME** ON THIS GLOBAL WARMING NONSENSE!

FORTUNATELY **SOME** LAWMAKERS AGREE! IN NORTH CAROLINA, THEY'VE PASSED A LAW **BANNING** STATE AGENCIES FROM BASING COASTAL POLICY ON PREDICTIONS OF SEA LEVEL CHANGE!

AND HOUSE REPUBLICANS JUST PASSED A BILL THAT WOULD RESTRICT THE **N.O.A.A.'S*** RESEARCH INTO SO-CALLED CLIMATE CHANGE!

IF THERE'S ONE THING RIGHT WING SCIENCE TEACHES US--IT'S THAT A PROBLEM **IGNORED** IS A PROBLEM **SOLVED**!

FOR NOW.

NOT THAT THERE'S ANY PROBLEM.

*NATIONAL OCEANIC AND ATMOSPHERIC ADMINISTRATION

AND WITH FEWER DISTRACTIONS, MAYBE WE CAN FOCUS OUR BIG-THINKING **SCIENCE BRAINS** ON **IMPORTANT** ISSUES--LIKE THE TRUTH ABOUT **BENGHAZI**! OR TAX CUTS FOR OUR FRIENDS THE **KOCH BROTHERS**!

BUT MISTER SCIENCE DUDE--

--ALMOST **ALL** SCIENTISTS AGREE THAT CLIMATE CHANGE IS **REAL** AND HAPPENING **NOW**--AND WILL HAVE **DEVASTATING CONSEQUENCES**!

OH, YOU CAN'T TRUST **THOSE** SCIENTISTS! **THEY** HAVE **ULTERIOR** MOTIVES-- UNLIKE FREE-THINKING, KOCH-FUNDED SKEPTICS SUCH AS **MYSELF**!

BUT THAT DOESN'T--

ZIP IT.

OKAY THEN! THAT'S ALL THE SCIENCE STUFF WE HAVE TIME FOR **TODAY**! TUNE IN NEXT WEEK FOR A LOOK AT **EVOLUTION**--MALICIOUS **HOAX** OR PERNICIOUS **LIE**?

SKEPTICAL FREE-THINKERS JUST WANT TO HAVE A **DEBATE**!

ALSO--WILL OBAMACARE USHER IN THE **APOCA-LYPSE**?

WE'LL LOOK AT THE **SCIENCE**!

TOM TOMORROW ©2014

THIS MODERN WORLD

by TOM TOMORROW

WELCOME BACK TO ACTION McNEWS NETWORK'S COMPREHENSIVE 24/7 COVERAGE OF THE **MYSTERIOUS DISAPPEARANCE**--

--OF **DEMOCRACY** IN THE **UNITED STATES**!

DEMOCRACY'S PATH HAS BEEN ERRATIC FOR QUITE AWHILE--AND NOW IT APPEARS TO HAVE GONE OFF THE MAP **ENTIRELY**!

PATRIOT ACT

CITIZENS UNITED

McCUTCHEON

?

CORRESPONDENT BETTY McBEDDIE JOINS US LIVE FROM THE **SEARCH ZONE**!

BIFF, WANDA--I'M HERE AT THE VENETIAN CASINO IN **LAS VEGAS**, WHERE REPUBLICAN PRESIDENTIAL HOPEFULS RECENTLY GATHERED TO GENUFLECT BEFORE BILLIONAIRE **SHELDON ADELSON**!

I'M SORRY TO SAY THERE'S NO SIGN OF DEMOCRACY **HERE**!

THANKS, BETTY!

THE SEARCH EXTENDS TO WASHINGTON D.C.--WHERE THE SUPREME COURT JUST DECLARED THAT **CAMPAIGN CONTRIBUTIONS** ARE A FORM OF **FREE SPEECH**!

HERE'S A SCALE **MODEL** OF THE SUPREME COURT FOR VIEWERS WHO MAY BE UNFAMILIAR WITH IT!

THERE ARE A LOT OF **CRAZY THEORIES** OUT THERE, BIFF! **SOME** PEOPLE ARE ASKING IF DEMOCRACY HAS SIMPLY BEEN **REPLACED**--BY **OLIGARCHY**!

OTHERS WONDER IF IT WAS SUCKED INTO A **BLACK HOLE**!

I GUESS **ANYTHING'S** POSSIBLE!

COMING UP NEXT: A BILLIONAIRE WHO SAYS EVERYTHING IS **FINE**!

THE RICH AND POOR ARE **EQUALLY FREE** TO PURCHASE POLITICAL INFLUENCE!

FIRST THESE MESSAGES!

ALSO: WE STILL DON'T KNOW WHAT HAPPENED TO THAT **PLANE**.

NO POINT IN SPECULATING! WHEN WE HAVE SOME NEWS, WE'LL TELL YOU.

THIS MODERN WORLD

by TOM TOMORROW

Rancher Bundy and his cows in "A Visit to the Big Apple"

THERE IT IS GIRLS--THE **EMPIRE STATE BUILDING!** YOU EVER **SEEN** ANYTHING SO TALL?

'COURSE YOU AIN'T. YOU'RE **COWS.**

LET'S GO TO THE **TOP!**

MOO.

MOOO.

BUT **THEN--**

SIR, YOU CAN'T BRING YOUR COWS INTO THE EMPIRE STATE BUILDING! IT'S AGAINST THE **RULES!**

SON, I LOVE THIS COUNTRY TOO MUCH TO BE HOGTIED BY YOUR SO-CALLED "RULES."

MY COWS AND I GO WHERE WE **PLEASE.**

MOOO.

RANCHER BUNDY'S HEAVILY-ARMED MILITIA BUDDIES QUICKLY RALLY TO HIS SIDE!

WE ARE PROUD PATRIOTS, HERE TO DEFEND **FREEDOM!**

AND COWS.

GIVE US WHAT WE WANT-- AND NOBODY GETS **HURT!**

FOX NEWS IS ON THE CASE!

WILL THIS TURN INTO ANOTHER VIOLENT CONFRONTATION WITH JACK-BOOTED GOVERNMENT **THUGS?**

THAT WOULD BE **TERRIBLE!**

EXCEPT FOR MY RATINGS.

STAY TUNED FOR **MORE** FROM THE NETWORK THAT LOVES AMERICA MORE THAN YOU.

FOX NEWS

UDDERLY OUTRAGEOUS
DID POLICE MIS-COW-CULATE?

LAW ENFORCEMENT BACKS DOWN.

WHEN FLAG-WAVING WHITE PEOPLE WITH GUNS DECIDE TO BREAK THE LAW--

--WHAT CAN YOU **DO?**

AND SO--

YOU GIRLS EVER SEEN A VIEW LIKE **THAT?**

'COURSE YOU AIN'T. YOU'RE **COWS.**

MOOO.

MOOO.

N E X T

WHADDYA SAY WE GO OUT TO THE **STATUE OF LIBERTY?**

MOO.

TOM TOMORROW ©2014

16

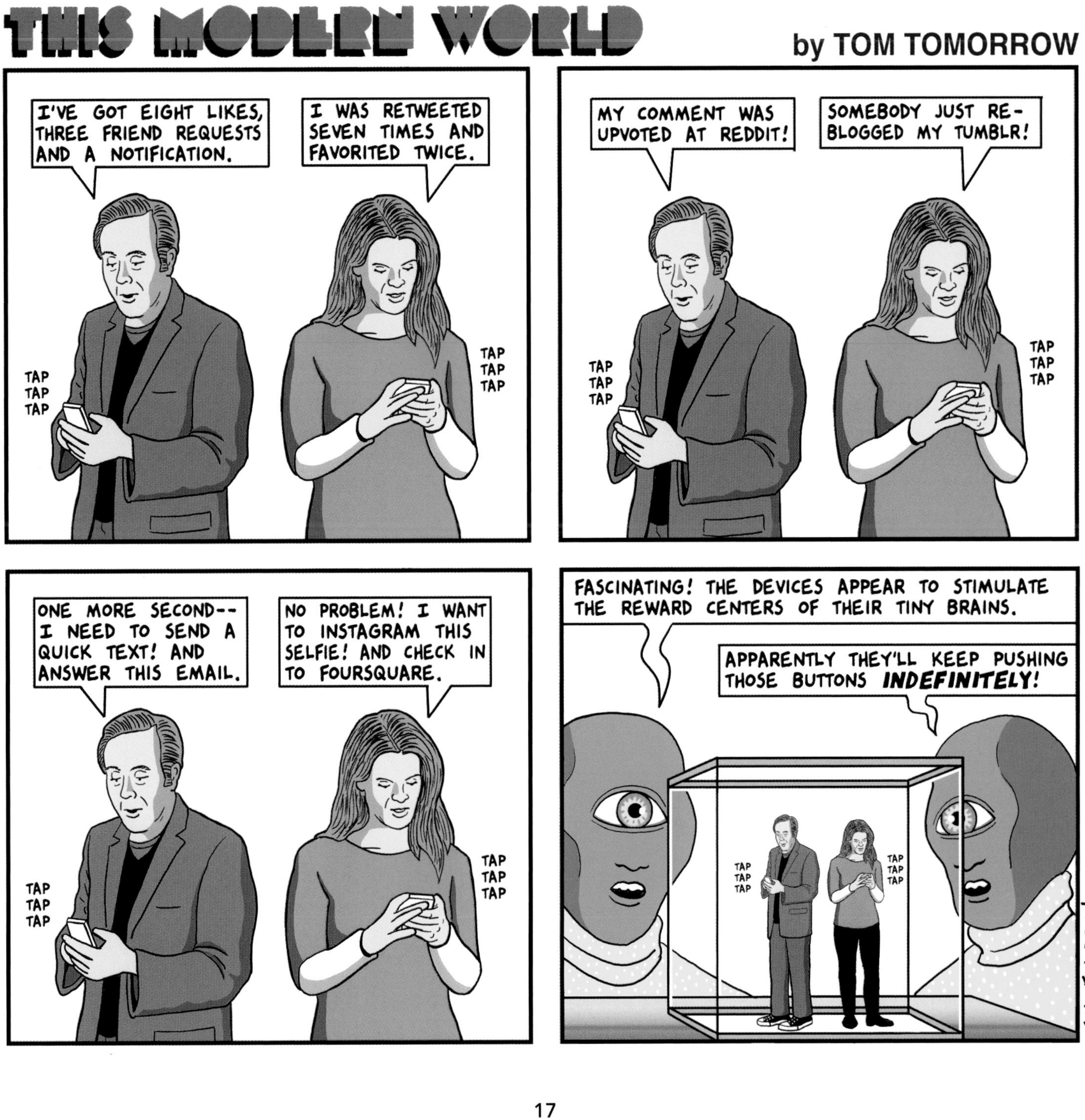
THIS MODERN WORLD
by TOM TOMORROW
I'VE GOT EIGHT LIKES, THREE FRIEND REQUESTS AND A NOTIFICATION.
TAP TAP TAP
I WAS RETWEETED SEVEN TIMES AND FAVORITED TWICE.
TAP TAP TAP
MY COMMENT WAS UPVOTED AT REDDIT!
TAP TAP TAP
SOMEBODY JUST RE-BLOGGED MY TUMBLR!
TAP TAP TAP
ONE MORE SECOND-- I NEED TO SEND A QUICK TEXT! AND ANSWER THIS EMAIL.
TAP TAP TAP
NO PROBLEM! I WANT TO INSTAGRAM THIS SELFIE! AND CHECK IN TO FOURSQUARE.
TAP TAP TAP
FASCINATING! THE DEVICES APPEAR TO STIMULATE THE REWARD CENTERS OF THEIR TINY BRAINS.
APPARENTLY THEY'LL KEEP PUSHING THOSE BUTTONS ***INDEFINITELY***!
TAP TAP TAP
TAP TAP TAP
TOM TOMORROW©2014

THIS MODERN WORLD

by TOM TOMORROW

JUSTICE IN AMERICA
with special guest host
McGRUFF THE CRIME DOG

HELLO, CHILDREN!

OUR TOPIC FOR TODAY IS *CAPITAL PUNISHMENT!*

YOU SEE, SOMETIMES A CRIMINAL DOES SOMETHING *SO BAD*, OUR FAIR AND IMPARTIAL JUSTICE SYSTEM HAS NO CHOICE BUT TO IMPOSE THE *ULTIMATE PENALTY.*

BUT SOMETIMES ONE OF THE DRUGS USED TO ADMINISTER THAT PENALTY BECOMES UNAVAILABLE--AND STATES LIKE OKLAHOMA HAVE TO SCRAMBLE TO FIND AN *UNTESTED ALTERNATIVE.*

?

AND *THEN* SOMETIMES, THINGS GO HORRIBLY WRONG AND THE PRISONER BEING EXECUTED REMAINS CONSCIOUS, CONVULSING ON THE GURNEY UNTIL HE ULTIMATELY DIES OF A MASSIVE *HEART ATTACK* FORTY MINUTES LATER.

AND THEN SOCIETY COLLECTIVELY RECOILS IN DISGUST AND REPEALS THE DEATH PENALTY ENTIRELY?

SURE, KID. AND I'M A REAL TALKING DOG.

TOM TOMORROW ©2014

18

THIS MODERN WORLD

by TOM TOMORROW

IT'S THE *LATEST* REPUBLICAN FOLK HERO--A *CARTOON HILLBILLY* WHO *HATES* THE GOVERNMENT!

GIT OFF MAH LAND, YOU DAD-GUM *REVENOOERS!*

RIGHT-WING MEDIA EMBRACE HIM *UNCRITICALLY!*

WHY CAIN'T THE GUB'MINT LEAVE A MAN ALONE TO BREW HISSELF SOME MOONSHINE IN *PEACE?*

I'VE OFTEN WONDERED THAT *MYSELF!*

CONSERVATIVES RALLY TO HIS CAUSE!

I THINK THE CARTOON HILLBILLY IS THE *NEW FACE* OF THE REPUBLICAN PARTY!

I WONDER IF HE'S EVER CONSIDERED RUNNING FOR *OFFICE!*

BUT *THEN*--

DO YOU HAVE ANY *MORE* FOLKSY, HOMESPUN WISDOM TO SHARE WITH US, CARTOON HILLBILLY?

WELL--I DON'T LIKE THE *BLACKS!* JEWS, NEITHER!

URK.

AND IT'S TIME TO QUICKLY CHANGE THE SUBJECT ONCE AGAIN.

IN *OTHER* NEWS--BENGHAZI, BENGHAZI, *BENGHAZI!*

ALSO, HILLARY CLINTON.

AND BENGHAZI.

NEXT: REPUBLICANS FIND A *NEW* CHAMPION--A CARTOON *CAVEMAN* WHO HATES *EVERYONE!*

OOG WANT TO SMASH ENEMIES WITH *CLUB!* TAKE THEIR *FOOD!* AND *WOMEN!*

I KNOW *EXACTLY* WHAT YOU MEAN!

TOM TOMORROW ©2014

THIS MODERN WORLD

by TOM TOMORROW

WHEN GUNS ARE EVERYWHERE ONLY PEOPLE WITH GUNS WILL HAVE GUNS

HELLO THERE! I SEE YOU'RE CARRYING A FIREARM--AS AM *I*!

IT *IS* OUR RIGHT AS CITIZENS OF A STATE WITH UNRESTRICTED OPEN-CARRY LAWS!

SOME MIGHT EVEN SAY, OUR *DUTY*!

BUT--HOW DO I KNOW *YOU'RE* A RESPONSIBLE GUN OWNER SUCH AS MYSELF--AND NOT A DISGRUNTLED EMPLOYEE HEADING FOR A FORMER *WORKPLACE*?

I COULD EASILY ASK THE SAME OF *YOU*!

FOR ALL *I* KNOW, YOU COULD BE A DERANGED SOCIOPATH ON YOUR WAY TO THE NEAREST *ELEMENTARY SCHOOL* OR *MOVIE THEATRE*!

SUCH UNCERTAINTY *MAY* JUST BE THE PRICE WE PAY--FOR *FREEDOM*!

PERHAPS YOU ARE CORRECT.

BAM!
BAM!

STILL, BETTER SAFE THAN SORRY.

EXCUSE ME--ARE YOU A *GOOD* GUY WITH A GUN--OR A *BAD* GUY WITH A GUN?

WHO WANTS TO *KNOW*?

TOM TOMORROW ©2014

20

THIS MODERN WORLD

by TOM TOMORROW

Conservative Jones, Boy Detective

and the Mystery of the Unhinged Netizens

MOONBAT! YOU'RE JUST IN TIME! I WAS JUST ATTEMPTING TO ASCERTAIN WHY CERTAIN INTERNET USERS ARE SO IRRATIONALLY ATTACHED TO THE NOTION OF *NET NEUTRALITY!*

OOOH, I KNOW *THIS* ONE!

UNDER NET NEUTRALITY, INTERNET SERVICE PROVIDERS MUST TREAT EVERYTHING THAT PASSES THROUGH THEIR NETWORKS EQUALLY--FROM AMAZON AND EBAY TO *YOUR BLOG.*

WITHOUT NET NEUTRALITY, ISP'S CAN CONTROL WHAT CONTENT WE CAN ACCESS, AND AT WHAT SPEED! THE OPEN INTERNET WILL BE A THING OF THE *PAST!*

OH, MOONBAT--

--WHAT'S IT *LIKE* TO LIVE IN THAT MARVELOUS FANTASY WORLD OF YOURS? DO MAGICAL UNICORNS FROLIC IN FIELDS OF LOLLIPOPS AND CANDY CANES, WHEN THEY'RE NOT BUSY STUDYING THE WORK OF *THOMAS PIKETTY?*

NO, THE ANSWER IS QUITE SIMPLE--

--NET NEUTRALITY ADVOCATES *HATE THE FREE MARKET!*

THAT'S ALWAYS YOUR ANSWER.

QUIET, MOONBAT! I'M WORKING ON A *NEW* MYSTERY--

--*WHY* DO SO MANY SCIENTISTS CLAIM TO BELIEVE IN *GLOBAL WARMING?*

NEXT: *AHA!* IT'S BECAUSE THEY *HATE THE FREE MARKET!*

THERE'S A SURPRISE.

TOM TOMORROW ©2014

THIS MODERN WORLD

by TOM TOMORROW

MISOGYNY.

WHY ARE WOMEN SUCH CONTEMPTIBLE, DUPLICITIOUS CREATURES?

AND **HOW** CAN WE TRICK THEM INTO HAVING SEX WITH US?

GUNS.

WHY DO PEOPLE OBJECT WHEN WE BRANDISH FIREARMS IN CHAIN RESTAURANTS?

HAVE THEY NOT **HEARD** OF THE SECOND AMENDMENT?

AND THEIR LETHAL CONFLUENCE.

"I WILL HAVE MY REVENGE...I WILL SLAUGHTER EVERY BLONDE SLUT I **SEE!**"*

*QUOTE FROM ELLIOTT RODGER'S LAST VIDEO

IT COULD HAVE BEEN A SOBERING MOMENT OF INTROSPECTION FOR PROPONENTS OF BOTH--

WOULD FEWER PEOPLE HAVE DIED IF NOT FOR THE EASY AVAILABILITY OF GUNS IN OUR SOCIETY?

AND **DID** THE TOXIC CULTURE OF ONLINE MISOGYNY FUEL THESE VIOLENT FANTASIES?

COUGH.

--BUT WHAT WERE THE ODDS OF THAT?

THESE HASHTAG FEMINAZIS WANT TO TAKE AWAY OUR GUNS--IF NOT OUR VERY **MANHOOD!**

CLEARLY **WE** ARE THE **TRUE** VICTIMS HERE.

ALSO, YARGLE BARGLE.

NOT TO MENTION, BLARGH.

TOM TOMORROW ©2014

SO OBAMA *CAN* IGNORE CONGRESS AND TRANSFER DETAINEES FROM GITMO?

WHEN CIRCUMSTANCES WARRANT.

GREAT! SO WHY DO WE STILL HAVE *ANYONE* IMPRISONED THERE--

--LET ALONE ALL THE MEN WHO FACE NO CHARGES AND HAVE BEEN CLEARED FOR RELEASE FOR *YEARS*?

BECAUSE RELEASING THEM WOULD NOT BE *PRACTICAL*!

THERE WOULD BE *MANY* DIFFICULTIES!

NOT TO MENTION *CHALLENGES*!

PERHAPS EVEN SOME *QUANDARIES*!

SO INSTEAD WE SHOULD JUST KEEP THEM LOCKED UP UNTIL THEY ROT AWAY AND *DIE*?

IT'S THE POLITICALLY EXPEDIENT THING TO DO.

TOM TOMORROW ©2014

THIS MODERN WORLD

by TOM TOMORROW

THE ANTI-PARTY

ANTI-SCIENCE.
CLIMATE CHANGE IS JUST A *THEORY!*

AS OPPOSED TO THE BIBLE, WHICH IS GOD'S LITERAL TRUTH.

ANTI-GOVERNMENT.
I DESPISE IT WITH A BURNING PASSION!

SO VOTE FOR *ME*-- AND I PROMISE TO DO AS TERRIBLE A JOB RUNNING IT AS *POSSIBLE!*

ANTI-HEALTH CARE.
WE WILL REPEAL OBAMA-CARE AND REPLACE IT WITH *OUR* PLAN--

--WHICH IS *NO* OBAMACARE!

ANTI-GUN VICTIM.
YOUR DEAD KIDS DON'T TRUMP *MY* CONSTITUTIONAL RIGHTS!

NEITHER DO YOUR DEAD POLICE OFFICERS.

OR YOUR DEAD RANDOM CIVILIANS.

OR YOUR--

ANTI-WOMAN.
CHICKS *DIG* GUYS WHO WANT TO TAKE AWAY THEIR RE-PRODUCTIVE RIGHTS!

AMIRITE, LADIES?

ANTI-IMMIGRANT.
IF WE DON'T WATCH OUT THIS COUNTRY WILL BE *OVERRUN* BY TIRED, POOR, HUDDLED MASSES!

LET THE WRETCHED REFUSE STAY ON THEIR *OWN* DAMN TEEMING SHORES!

ANTI-P.O.W.
IF BERGDAHL WAS A DE-SERTER--HE SHOULD HAVE BEEN LEFT WITH THE TALIBAN TO *DIE!*

I THINK THAT'S IN THE UNI-FORM CODE OF MILITARY JUSTICE.

ANTI-MINORITY.
NONSENSE! "RACE HUSTLERS" WHO ALWAYS BRING UP THE "RACE CARD" ARE THE *REAL* RACISTS!

UNLIKE OPPRESSED VICTIMS SUCH AS OURSELVES.

ANTI-GAY.
I *DEMAND* THAT SOCIETY RESPECT MY DEEPLY HELD RELIGIOUS CONVICTION--

--THAT GAY SEX IS ICKY.

ANTI-POOR.
"NO ONE HAS THE GUTS TO JUST LET THEM WITHER AND *DIE!*"*

*A THING THAT WAS AC-TUALLY SAID BY A G.O.P. CANDIDATE IN INDIANA.

ANTI-REALITY.
THE IRAQ WAR WAS AN UNPARALLELED *SUCCESS*--UNTIL *OBAMA* TOOK OVER!

THAT'S OUR STORY AND WE'RE STICKING TO IT.

TOM TOMORROW ©2014

24

THIS MODERN WORLD

by TOM TOMORROW

BILL KRISTOL--HOW DO **YOU** THINK WE SHOULD RESPOND TO THE SITUATION IN IRAQ?

CLEARLY WE MUST SEND OUR FORCES **BACK**--AND KEEP THEM THERE AS LONG AS **NECESSARY!**

I **SEE!** NOW, JUST TO PUT THINGS IN PERSPECTIVE FOR THE VIEWERS AT HOME--YOU WERE ONE OF THE EARLIEST **PROPONENTS** OF THE INVASION OF IRAQ--

--DECLARING THAT IT WOULD ONLY LAST **TWO MONTHS**--AND WE WOULD BE GREETED AS **LIBERATORS!**

YOU ALSO SAID THERE WAS "ALMOST NO EVIDENCE" THAT "THE SHIA CAN'T GET ALONG WITH THE SUNNI!"

AND THAT "THE BATTLES OF IRAQ AND AFGHANISTAN" HAD BEEN "WON DECISIVELY"--IN **APRIL 2003!**

THE POINT IS, WE WANT TO **THANK** YOU FOR SHARING YOUR OPINION ON THE CURRENT CRISIS--

--SO EVERYONE KNOWS **EXACTLY** WHAT **NOT** TO DO!

OH, AND JUST FOR GOOD MEASURE--

--WE'VE DEVELOPED THE TECHNOLOGY TO BANISH YOU TO AN INTERDIMENSIONAL REALM WHERE YOU'LL BE CONDEMNED TO SPEND ETERNITY LOCKED IN MORTAL COMBAT WITH YOUR **ANTI-MATTER** SELF!

WAIT, WHAT?

BUH **BYE!**

BZAPP!

FOLKS, THIS HAS BEEN AN ILLUSTRATION OF WHAT **WOULD** HAPPEN, IF WE LIVED IN A JUST WORLD.

COMING UP NEXT: WHAT DOES **DICK CHENEY** THINK WE SHOULD DO IN IRAQ?

POP!

TOM TOMORROW ©2014

25

THIS MODERN WORLD

by TOM TOMORROW

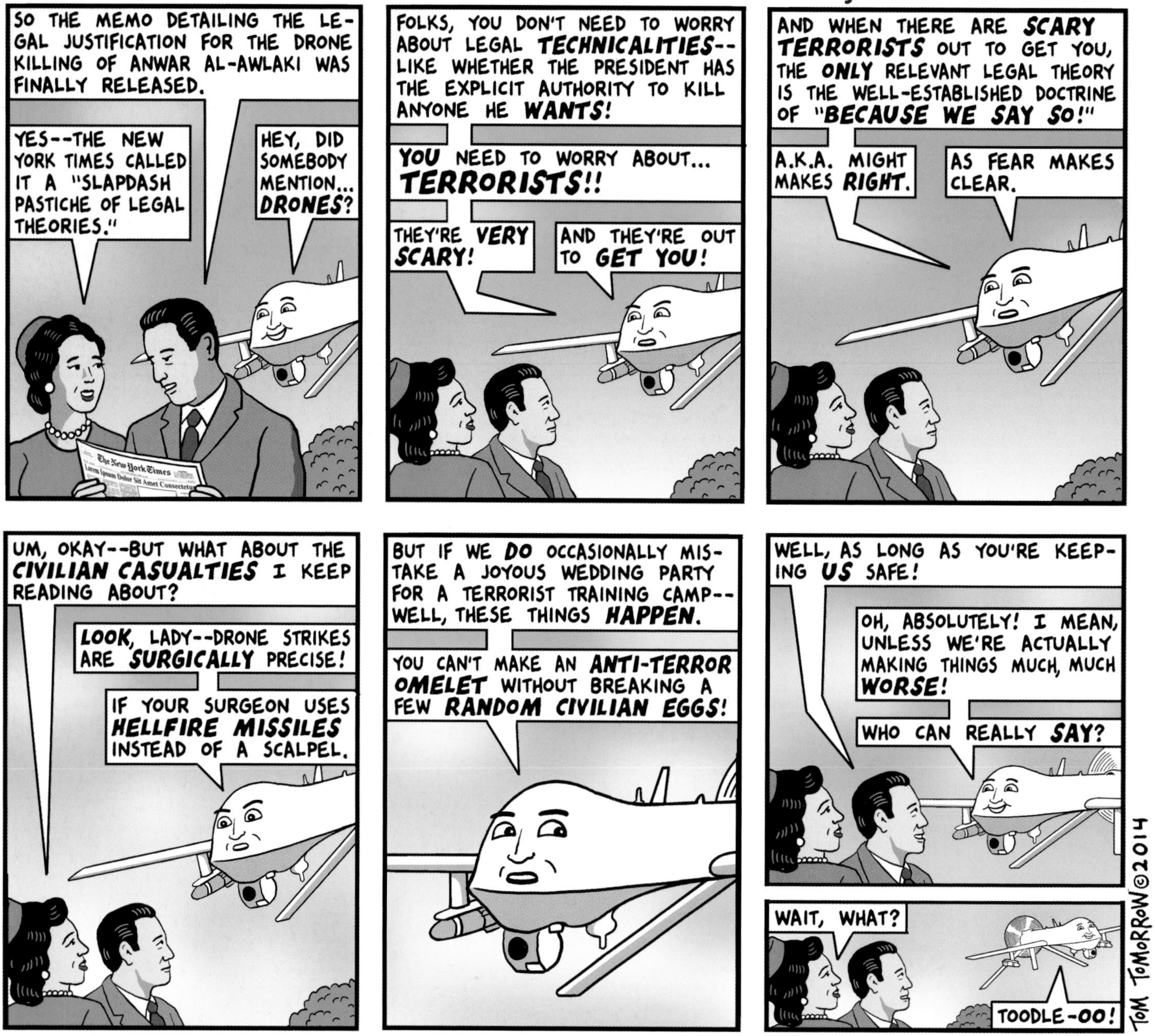

SO THE MEMO DETAILING THE LEGAL JUSTIFICATION FOR THE DRONE KILLING OF ANWAR AL-AWLAKI WAS FINALLY RELEASED.
YES--THE NEW YORK TIMES CALLED IT A "SLAPDASH PASTICHE OF LEGAL THEORIES."
HEY, DID SOMEBODY MENTION... DRONES?
The New York Times
Lorem Ipsum Dolor Sit Amet Consectetur
FOLKS, YOU DON'T NEED TO WORRY ABOUT LEGAL TECHNICALITIES--LIKE WHETHER THE PRESIDENT HAS THE EXPLICIT AUTHORITY TO KILL ANYONE HE WANTS!
YOU NEED TO WORRY ABOUT... TERRORISTS!!
THEY'RE VERY SCARY!
AND THEY'RE OUT TO GET YOU!
AND WHEN THERE ARE SCARY TERRORISTS OUT TO GET YOU, THE ONLY RELEVANT LEGAL THEORY IS THE WELL-ESTABLISHED DOCTRINE OF "BECAUSE WE SAY SO!"
A.K.A. MIGHT MAKES RIGHT.
AS FEAR MAKES CLEAR.
UM, OKAY--BUT WHAT ABOUT THE CIVILIAN CASUALTIES I KEEP READING ABOUT?
LOOK, LADY--DRONE STRIKES ARE SURGICALLY PRECISE!
IF YOUR SURGEON USES HELLFIRE MISSILES INSTEAD OF A SCALPEL.
BUT IF WE DO OCCASIONALLY MISTAKE A JOYOUS WEDDING PARTY FOR A TERRORIST TRAINING CAMP--WELL, THESE THINGS HAPPEN.
YOU CAN'T MAKE AN ANTI-TERROR OMELET WITHOUT BREAKING A FEW RANDOM CIVILIAN EGGS!
WELL, AS LONG AS YOU'RE KEEPING US SAFE!
OH, ABSOLUTELY! I MEAN, UNLESS WE'RE ACTUALLY MAKING THINGS MUCH, MUCH WORSE!
WHO CAN REALLY SAY?
WAIT, WHAT?
TOODLE-OO!
TOM TOMORROW©2014

THIS MODERN WORLD

by TOM TOMORROW

IT'S OFFICIAL--CORPORATIONS ARE **RELIGIOUS** PEOPLE!

*I AM A **VERY** DEVOUT HOBBY AND CRAFT STORE!*

THE RULING CAME IN THE LANDMARK LEGAL CASE OF "*SCIENCE V. SUPERSTITION.*"

THIS COURT FINDS THAT THE HEALTH CARE NEEDS OF WOMEN ARE **OUT-WEIGHED**--

--BY THE IMAGINED PREFERENCES OF AN **INVISIBLE SKY GOD**!

THOUGH THE JUSTICES WERE QUICK TO INSIST THAT NO **PRECEDENT** HAD BEEN SET.

THIS DECISION IS SPECIFICALLY LIMITED TO **CHRISTIAN** CORPORATIONS AND THEIR OPPOSITION TO FORMS OF BIRTH CONTROL THEY MISTAKENLY BELIEVE TO BE ABORTIFACIENTS.

OTHER RELIGIONS NEED NOT **APPLY**!

IT DEFINITELY HIGHLIGHTED THE ODD AMERICAN LINKAGE OF HEALTH CARE TO **EMPLOYMENT STATUS**.

A WOMAN'S REPRODUCTIVE HEALTH IS BETWEEN HER AND HER DOCTOR--

--AND THE BOSS AT HER CRAPPY CHAIN STORE JOB!

AS GOD **INTENDED**!

CONSERVATIVES CELEBRATED WITH AN **EXPLOSION** OF MISOGYNY.

TOO **BAD**, HARLOTS! NO MORE EMPLOYER-SUBSIDIZED NON-PRO-CREATIVE SEX FOR **YOU**!

IF YOU DON'T WANT BABIES, WHY DON'T YOU KEEP YOUR LEGS **CROSSED**--LIKE **DECENT** WOMENFOLK?

AND WHAT **BETTER** ELECTORAL STRATEGY COULD THERE **BE**--

--THAN TO DEMONIZE THE OVER-WHELMING MAJORITY OF WOMEN WHO HAVE USED **BIRTH CONTROL** AT SOME POINT IN THEIR LIVES?

THEIR SLUTTY SEX-HAVING DOESN'T TRUMP **MY** RELIGIOUS FAITH--OR MY GENERAL DISCOMFORT WITH FEMALE SEXUALITY!

THEY SHOULD CHANNEL THEIR EXCESS ENERGY INTO SOME SORT OF **HOBBY**--AND **I** KNOW JUST THE PLACE TO **GO**!

TOM TOMORROW ©2014

27

THIS MODERN WORLD

by TOM TOMORROW

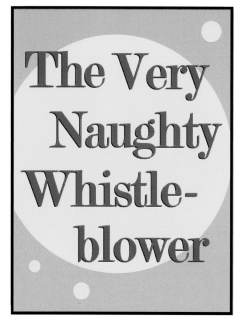

The Very Naughty Whistle-blower

ONCE UPON A TIME, A VERY NAUGHTY WHISTLEBLOWER REVEALED INFORMATION THE GOVERNMENT DID NOT WANT REVEALED.

THEY'RE SPYING ON *EVERYONE!*

OH, I REALLY WISH YOU HADN'T DONE THAT.

ER, I MEAN, I *WELCOME* THIS DEBATE.

THE CITIZENS OF THE LAND WERE OUTRAGED, AND HAD MUCH TO SAY-- ABOUT THE WHISTLEBLOWER'S POSSIBLE *CHARACTER DEFECTS*, THAT IS!*

WE *MIGHT* BE MORE CONCERNED ABOUT THE PERVASIVE SURVEILLANCE STATE HE HAS EXPOSED--

--IF HE WERE A MORE *LIKABLE PERSON!*

*NOT TO MENTION THOSE OF THE JOURNALISTS HE WORKED WITH!

A YEAR LATER, GOVERNMENT OFFICIALS CONTINUED TO DENOUNCE HIM!

IF THE NAUGHTY WHISTLEBLOWER HAS SOMETHING TO *SAY*, HE SHOULD COME HOME AND FACE A TRIAL WHERE HE WON'T BE ALLOWED TO SAY IT DUE TO ESPIONAGE ACT RESTRICTIONS!

THE EFFEMINATE *COWARD!*

MAINSTREAM PUNDITS EXPRESSED *THEIR* DISDAIN!

WE CAN'T ALLOW NAUGHTY WHISTLE-BLOWERS TO CONTROL THE RELEASE OF INFORMATION THE GOVERNMENT DOES NOT WANT REVEALED!

THE *GOVERNMENT* MUST BE IN CHARGE OF *THAT!*

MEANWHILE...

HOW ARE WE DOING? DO CITIZENS THINK HE IS A *HERO* OR A *ZERO?*

I DON'T KNOW SIR. I'LL CHECK THEIR EMAIL, PHONE RECORDS, BROWSER HISTORIES, AND METADATA--AND GET *BACK* TO YOU!

TOM TOMORROW©2014

THIS MODERN WORLD
by TOM TOMORROW

BREAKING NEWS

FOUR YOUNG BOYS WERE KILLED BY ISRAELI ROCKETS WHILE PLAYING SOCCER ON THE BEACH IN GAZA.

HUNDREDS OF PALESTINIAN CIVILIANS HAVE LOST THEIR LIVES IN THE CURRENT BOMBARDMENT--

--AND WITH THE GROUND OFFENSIVE UNDERWAY, THE NUMBERS ARE ONLY EX-PECTED TO *RISE*.

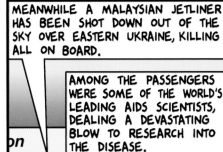

MEANWHILE A MALAYSIAN JETLINER HAS BEEN SHOT DOWN OUT OF THE SKY OVER EASTERN UKRAINE, KILLING ALL ON BOARD.

AMONG THE PASSENGERS WERE SOME OF THE WORLD'S LEADING AIDS SCIENTISTS, DEALING A DEVASTATING BLOW TO RESEARCH INTO THE DISEASE.

IN A RELATED STORY, SOURCES SAY THE WORLD IS A DARK AND CHAOTIC PLACE, DEVOID OF MEANING OR HOPE, IN WHICH EVIL FREQUENTLY TRIUMPHS AND SOCIO-PATHIC BRUTALITY IS THE NORM.

HUMAN BEINGS ARE ADVISED TO FIND WHAT SMALL SOLACE THEY CAN BEFORE TRAGEDY INEVITABLY OVERWHELMS *THEIR* INSIGNIFICANT LIVES.

COUGH.

COMING UP NEXT: CAN YOU *BELIEVE* MARVEL COMICS HAS MADE THOR A *WOMAN*?

WE'LL TALK WITH SOME *OUTRAGED* FANS AFTER THESE MESSAGES!

Tom Tomorrow ©2014

29

THIS MODERN WORLD

by TOM TOMORROW

THE OVERWHELMING MAJORITY OF PEOPLE KILLED IN GAZA HAVE BEEN *CIVILIANS*--

--AND A LOT OF *THOSE* HAVE BEEN *CHILDREN!*

?

EXCUSE ME, KIDS--*I* KNOW A THING OR TWO ABOUT *CIVILIAN CASUALTIES!*

I MEAN TO SAY, I'VE--YOU KNOW-- READ *ARTICLES* AND STUFF.

*ANY*HOO--

--TAKE IT FROM *ME*--THERE'S *NO POINT* IN OBSESSING OVER A LITTLE *COLLATERAL DAMAGE!*

AND YOU *CERTAINLY* DON'T WANT TO WASTE TIME TRYING TO ASSIGN *BLAME.*

UNLESS YOU'RE BLAMING HAMAS.

BUT REALLY--THERE'S NO NEED FOR *YOU* TO WORRY ABOUT *ANY* OF THIS! THE *GROWN-UPS* WILL SORT THINGS OUT!

SOONER OR LATER.

ONE WAY OR ANOTHER.

MAYBE THE GROWNUPS COULD THINK ABOUT SORTING THINGS OUT WITHOUT KILLING ANY MORE *TEN YEAR OLDS.*

HA HA! SURE, AND MAYBE EVERYONE WILL GET A *FREE PONY!*

OH. YOU WEREN'T JOKING.

TOM TOMORROW ©2014

30

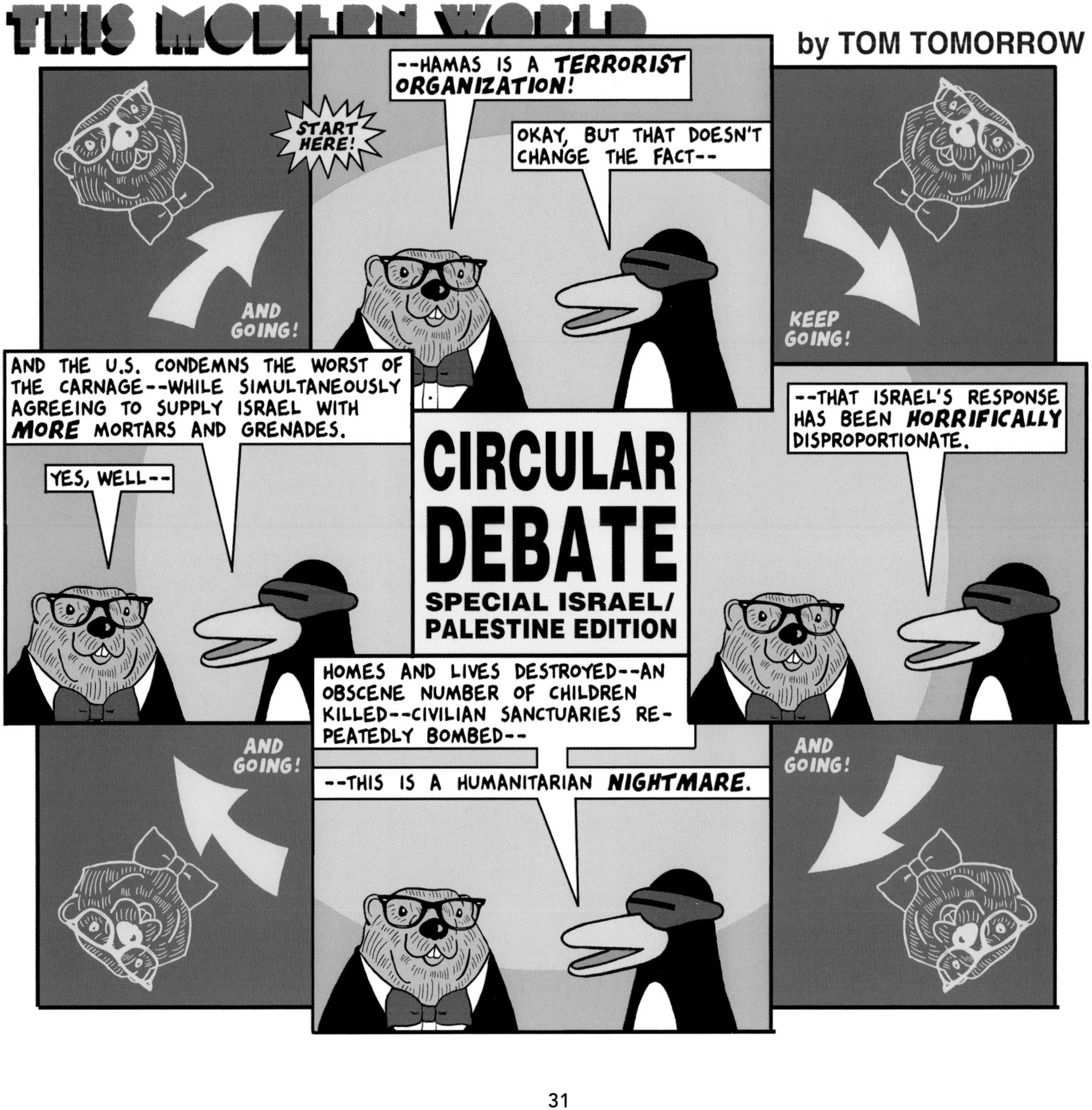
THIS MODERN WORLD
by TOM TOMORROW
CIRCULAR DEBATE
SPECIAL ISRAEL/ PALESTINE EDITION
START HERE!
--HAMAS IS A TERRORIST ORGANIZATION!
OKAY, BUT THAT DOESN'T CHANGE THE FACT--
KEEP GOING!
--THAT ISRAEL'S RESPONSE HAS BEEN HORRIFICALLY DISPROPORTIONATE.
AND GOING!
HOMES AND LIVES DESTROYED--AN OBSCENE NUMBER OF CHILDREN KILLED--CIVILIAN SANCTUARIES REPEATEDLY BOMBED--
--THIS IS A HUMANITARIAN NIGHTMARE.
AND GOING!
YES, WELL--
AND THE U.S. CONDEMNS THE WORST OF THE CARNAGE--WHILE SIMULTANEOUSLY AGREEING TO SUPPLY ISRAEL WITH MORE MORTARS AND GRENADES.
AND GOING!

THIS MODERN WORLD

by TOM TOMORROW

PRESS CONFERENCE

WE TORTURED SOME FOLKS.

AND THE ONLY GOVERNMENT OFFICIAL WHO WENT TO JAIL FOR IT WAS THE WHISTLEBLOWER WHO EXPOSED IT.

BUT LET'S NOT GET *SANCTIMONIOUS!*

BRAVE PATRIOTS WORKING UNDER PRESSURE MADE *MISTAKES.*

LET HE AMONG US WHO HASN'T ACCIDENTALLY WATERBOARDED SOMEONE CAST THE FIRST *STONE!*

I MEAN, SURE, FINE -- WE TORTURED A *LOT* OF FOLKS.

AND RENDERED MORE TO OTHER COUNTRIES TO *BE* TORTURED.

AND IT WAS ALL SANCTIONED AT THE HIGHEST LEVELS OF GOVERNMENT.

BUT NOT TO WORRY! ONE OF THE FIRST THINGS *I* DID WAS BAN *SOME* OF THOSE ENHANCED INTERROGATION TECHNIQUES!

YES, I SAID "SOME."*

AHEM.

*HE REALLY DID!

STILL, WE *MUST* ACCEPT RESPONSIBILITY! WHICH IS TO SAY, WE MUST BRIEFLY ACKNOWLEDGE THE UNPLEASANTNESS IN THE UPCOMING TORTURE REPORT, AND THEN QUICKLY MOVE ON.

AND -- WE SHOULD *REALLY* TRY NOT TO TORTURE ANY *MORE* FOLKS IN THE *FUTURE!*

IF ONLY THERE WERE SOME SORT OF -- I DON'T KNOW -- LEGAL *CONSEQUENCES* TO *DETER* PEOPLE FROM COMMITTING SUCH ACTS!

OH WELL! WHAT CAN YOU *DO?*

TOM TOMORROW©2014

THIS MODERN WORLD

by TOM TOMORROW

OFFICER FRIENDLY, WHY ARE YOU DRESSED LIKE *DARTH VADER*?

IS IT *HAL-LOWEEN* ALREADY?

HEH HEH! NO, KIDS--I'M JUST DOING MY *JOB*!

YOU SEE, LOCAL POLICE GET ALL *KINDS* OF SURPLUS EQUIPMENT FROM THE MILITARY THESE DAYS-- FROM ASSAULT RIFLES TO THIRTY-TON *COMBAT VEHICLES*!

BUT WHY DO YOU *WANT* ALL THAT STUFF?

BECAUSE IT'S *COOL*!

I MEAN, TO KEEP YOU SAFE.

BUT HASN'T THE MILITARIZATION OF POLICE WORK REPEATEDLY LED TO *TRAGEDY*--LIKE WHEN A SWAT TEAM KILLED A 68-YEAR-OLD *GRANDFATHER* DURING A BOTCHED DRUG RAID?

OR WHEN A *TWO-YEAR-OLD* HAD A FLASH-BANG GRENADE GO OFF IN HIS *CRIB*?

LET *ALONE* THE POLICE RESPONSE TO PROTESTERS IN *FERGUSON*! IT'S BEEN LOOKING LIKE AN *OCCUPATION* THERE!

IF YOU *HAVE* ALL THIS MILITARY EQUIPMENT--

--AREN'T YOU JUST GOING TO LOOK FOR AN EXCUSE TO *USE* IT?

ARE YOU POTENTIAL RIOTERS GOING TO *DISPERSE*--OR DO I NEED TO CALL FOR AN *ARMORED COMBAT VEHICLE*?

WE WERE JUST LEAVING.

PLEASE DON'T SHOOT US.

TOM TOMORROW ©2014

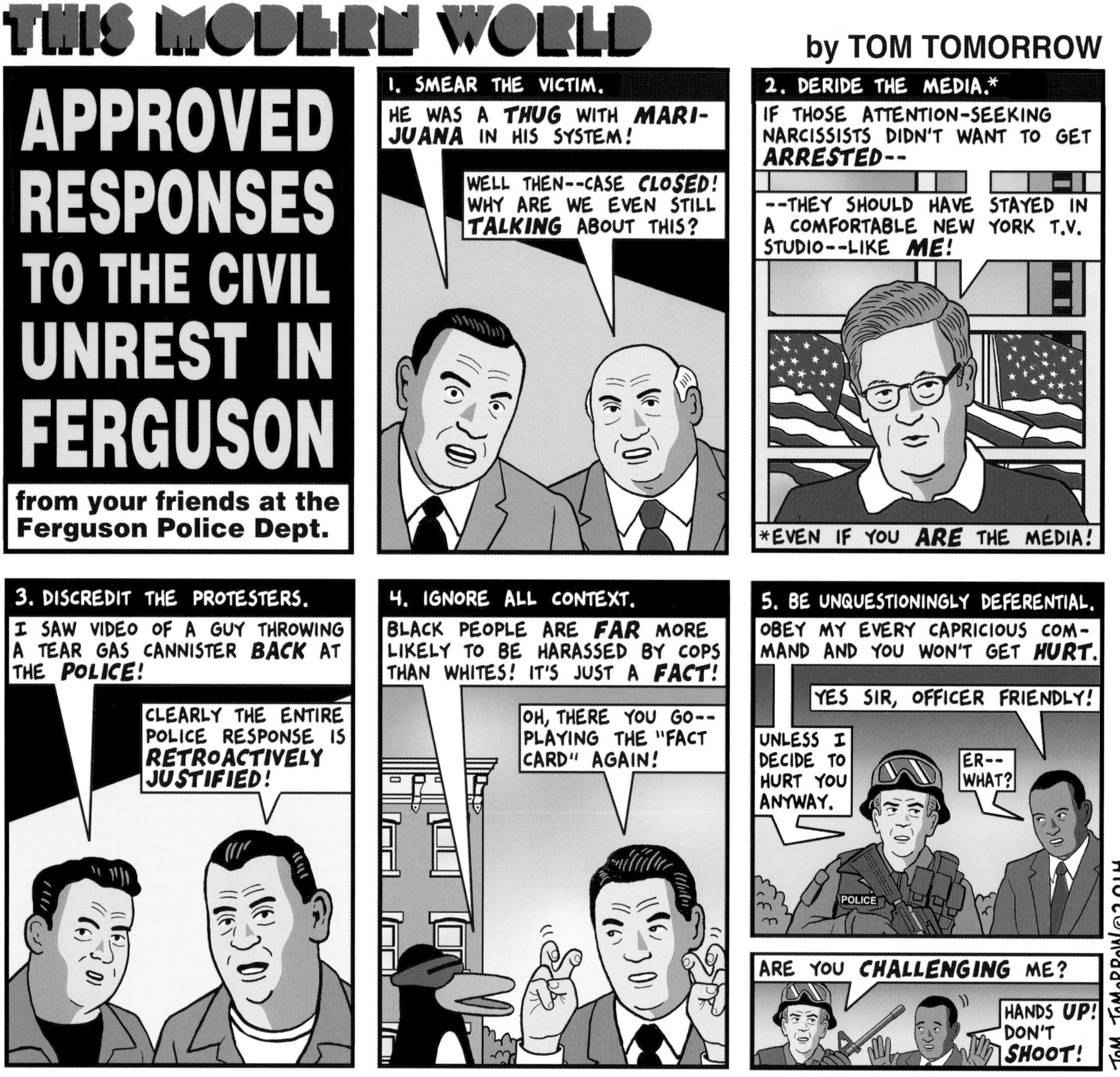
THIS MODERN WORLD
by TOM TOMORROW
APPROVED RESPONSES TO THE CIVIL UNREST IN FERGUSON
from your friends at the Ferguson Police Dept.
1. SMEAR THE VICTIM.
HE WAS A THUG WITH MARIJUANA IN HIS SYSTEM!
WELL THEN--CASE CLOSED! WHY ARE WE EVEN STILL TALKING ABOUT THIS?
2. DERIDE THE MEDIA.*
IF THOSE ATTENTION-SEEKING NARCISSISTS DIDN'T WANT TO GET ARRESTED--
--THEY SHOULD HAVE STAYED IN A COMFORTABLE NEW YORK T.V. STUDIO--LIKE ME!
*EVEN IF YOU ARE THE MEDIA!
3. DISCREDIT THE PROTESTERS.
I SAW VIDEO OF A GUY THROWING A TEAR GAS CANNISTER BACK AT THE POLICE!
CLEARLY THE ENTIRE POLICE RESPONSE IS RETROACTIVELY JUSTIFIED!
4. IGNORE ALL CONTEXT.
BLACK PEOPLE ARE FAR MORE LIKELY TO BE HARASSED BY COPS THAN WHITES! IT'S JUST A FACT!
OH, THERE YOU GO--PLAYING THE "FACT CARD" AGAIN!
5. BE UNQUESTIONINGLY DEFERENTIAL.
OBEY MY EVERY CAPRICIOUS COMMAND AND YOU WON'T GET HURT.
YES SIR, OFFICER FRIENDLY!
UNLESS I DECIDE TO HURT YOU ANYWAY.
ER-- WHAT?
POLICE
ARE YOU CHALLENGING ME?
HANDS UP! DON'T SHOOT!
TOM TOMORROW©2014

THIS MODERN WORLD

by TOM TOMORROW

WELL, IT APPEARS THAT FORMER VICE PRESIDENT **DICK CHENEY** AND HIS FAMILY ARE **LATE** FOR OUR SCHEDULED **INTERVIEW**--

OH, WAIT!

SORRY--

--WE WERE TORMENTING LOST SOULS IN THE LAKE OF ETERNAL DAMNATION. LOST TRACK OF THE TIME.

HA HA! AND THEY SAY YOU DON'T HAVE A SENSE OF HUMOR, SIR!

I'M NOT JOKING.

UM, OKAY. **SO.** THE QUESTION ON EVERYONE'S MIND--**IRAQ!** DO YOU FEEL **ANY** RESPONSIBILITY FOR THE ONGOING CHAOS AND BLOODSHED, LET ALONE THE RISE OF **ISIS?**

WHAT??

FOOLISH **MORTAL!** HOW **DARE** YOU QUESTION THE LORD OF DARKNESS AND ALL THAT IS **VILE?** I SHOULD FLAY YOU **ALIVE** AND HANG YOUR WRITHING BODY ON A STAKE AS A WARNING TO ALL WHO PASS **BY!**

ER--I MEAN TO SAY, INVADING IRAQ WAS ABSOLUTELY THE RIGHT THING TO DO.

ALL RIGHT THEN! MOVING ALONG-- WHAT DOES THE CHENEY FAMILY THINK WE SHOULD DO ABOUT **CLIMATE CHANGE?**

NOTHING!

WE **LIKE** IT HOT!

TOM TOMORROW ©2014

35

THIS MODERN WORLD

BY TOM TOMORROW

CAPTAIN'S LOG: THE ENTERPRISE HAS TRAVELED BACK IN TIME TO A PRIMITIVE AND BARBARIC ERA IN EARTH'S HISTORY--THE YEAR 2014! OUR MISSION--*HISTORICAL RESEARCH!*

CAPTAIN, I'VE LINKED THE SHIP'S COMPUTERS TO THE PLANETARY DATA NETWORK--

--BUT IT'S CLOGGED WITH VITRIOL, SOPHISTRY, AND MISOGYNY! I'M HAVING TROUBLE LOCATING ANY USEFUL *INFORMATION!*

KEEP TRYING, LIEUTENANT. MR. SPOCK--REPORT.

I AM MONITORING A COMMUNICATIONS PLATFORM KNOWN AS "TWITTER"--WHERE I HAVE INADVERTENTLY BECOME INVOLVED IN A DISPUTE REGARDING THE POSSESSION OF *FIREARMS!*

FORTUNATELY I BELIEVE THAT USER @REDSTATEOPENCARRYGUNLUVVER26 IS RECEPTIVE TO *LOGIC* AND *REASON*--OR ELSE WHY WOULD HE OR SHE HAVE *INITIATED* THIS DEBATE?

COMPUTER--TRANSLATE THE 21ST CENTURY COLLOQUIALISM, "LIBTARD."

PRO-CESS-ING.

ENGINEERING TO BRIDGE! SOMEONE ON THE PLANET'S SURFACE IS TRYIN' TO HACK INTO OUR *MEMORY BANKS!*

LOCK THEM *OUT*, SCOTTY--BEFORE THEY LEARN SOMETHING THAT COULD...CHANGE...*HISTORY!*

AYE, SIR--BUT I DINNA THINK YOU NEED TO WORRY! THEY SEEM TO BE SEARCHING FOR--WELL--PICTURES OF NAKED WOMEN, SIR.

JIM, WHAT IN BLAZES WAS *WRONG* WITH THESE PEOPLE?

THEIR...*TECHNOLOGY*...OUTSTRIPPED THEIR...*MATURITY.* THEY BECAME *ADDICTED*...TO CONSTANT *STIMULATION* AND POINTLESS *DISTRACTION!*

IT'S A...*WONDER*...HUMANITY SURVIVED THE *CENTURY!*

MR. SULU--GET US *OUT* OF HERE!

SURE, CAPTAIN--AS SOON AS I UPLOAD THESE *CAT MEMES* I JUST MADE--TO SOMETHING CALLED *FACEBOOK!*

HEH! I MUST ADMIT...THEY *ARE* AMUSING!

BUT--WHY DOES THE CAT...*WANT*...DILITHIUM CRYSTALS?

NEXT: CAN THE CREW ESCAPE THE INSIDIOUS INFLUENCE OF THE 21ST CENTURY--BEFORE IT'S *TOO LATE*?

CAPTAIN--WHY IS THERE A *PENIS* ON THE MAIN VIEWSCREEN?

BLASTED TRICORDER! I WAS...*TRYING*...TO TEXT YEOMAN RAND!

TOM TOMORROW ©2014...WITH APOLOGIES TO SHATNER, NIMOY, NICHOLS, TAKEI, ET AL!

THIS MODERN WORLD

by TOM TOMORROW

building blocks of war

MEDIA FEARMONGERING.

COMING UP NEXT: ARE ISIS TERRORISTS HIDING UNDER **YOUR BED** WAITING FOR YOU TO FALL **ASLEEP?**

OUR EXPERTS SAY IT'S **POSSIBLE!**

POLITICAL GRANDSTANDING.

"THE THREAT ISIS POSES **CANNOT** BE OVERSTATED!" --DIANNE FEINSTEIN

"(OBAMA) NEEDS TO RISE TO THE OCCASION--BEFORE WE ALL GET **KILLED** BACK HERE AT HOME!" --LINDSEY GRAHAM

"(THEY) SAY THEY'RE GOING TO FLY THE BLACK FLAG OF ISIS OVER THE WHITE HOUSE...A CLEAR AND PRESENT **DANGER!**" --BILL NELSON

"WE HAVEN'T SEEN ANYTHING LIKE THIS SINCE HITLER AND THE **BLITZKRIEG!**" --MICHELE BACHMANN

PUBLIC HYSTERIA.

THIS IS THE SCARIEST THREAT WE HAVE FACED SINCE THE **LAST** SCARY THREAT!

WHAT CHOICE DO WE **HAVE,** BUT TO COMMIT OURSELVES TO ADDITIONAL YEARS OF WAR IN A REGION WE DON'T REALLY UNDERSTAND, AND IN WHICH WE HAVE NO RELIABLE ALLIES?

THIRTEEN-YEAR-OLD RETROFITTED LEGAL RATIONALE.

THE AUMF **TOTALLY** GIVES US THE AUTHORITY WE NEED!

I'LL SEE IF I CAN FIND THAT OLD "MISSION ACCOMPLISHED" BANNER--MAYBE WE CAN USE **IT** TOO!

AMBIGUOUS REASSURANCES.

WE WILL **DEFINITELY** NOT SEND AMERICAN TROOPS INTO COMBAT!

UNLESS WE HAVE TO.

WHICH WE PROBABLY WILL.

MANIC PIXIE DREAM INSURGENTS.

THEY WILL DO EXACTLY WHAT WE **WANT** THEM TO DO AND NOTHING MORE!

AND THEN THEY WILL POLITELY RETURN OUR WEAPONS AND EVERYONE WILL LIVE HAPPILY EVER AFTER.

SEMANTIC QUIBBLING.

IF WE ARE DROPPING BOMBS AND KILLING PEOPLE **WITHOUT** "BOOTS ON THE GROUND"--THEN IT IS **NOT** A "WAR"!

BECAUSE **REASONS!**

ETERNAL OPTIMISM.

WE MUST INTERVENE TO CLEAN UP THE MESS THAT AROSE OUT OF THE **LAST** MESS WE CREATED BY INTERVENING!

I'M **SURE** WE'LL GET IT RIGHT **THIS** TIME!

TOM TOMORROW ©2014

by TOM TOMORROW

SO HERE WE GO--BACK TO WAR IN IRAQ, AND SYRIA *TOO!* WHAT COULD GO WRONG?

WHAT CHOICE DO WE *HAVE?* ISIS MIGHT BE THE SCARIEST THREAT WE'VE EVER *FACED!*

THEY COULD HAVE SLEEPER CELLS ON AMERICAN SOIL AS WE *SPEAK!* AN ATTACK ON THE HOMELAND IS PROBABLY *IMMINENT!*

WELL, IF THEIR GOAL WAS TO TERRORIZE YOU, THEY DO SEEM TO HAVE SUCCEEDED.

YES, THEY'RE BAD PEOPLE WHO DO VERY BAD THINGS. BUT THEY'RE NOT JAMES BOND SUPERVILLAINS, AND THEY *REALLY* DON'T POSE AN EXISTENTIAL THREAT TO THE UNITED STATES OF AMERICA.

HMMPH.

YOU KNOW WHAT YOUR PROBLEM IS? YOU'RE IN *DENIAL!* YOU CAN'T SEE AN "EXISTENTIAL THREAT" TO OUR WAY OF LIFE WHEN IT'S STARING EVERY ONE OF US IN THE *FACE!*

SO ABOUT *CLIMATE CHANGE--*

IT'S A MYTH. HUMANS WILL ADAPT. NOTHING TO WORRY ABOUT.

THIS MODERN WORLD

by TOM TOMORROW

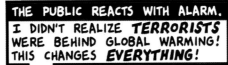

THE PRESIDENT MAKES AN UN-EXPECTED ANNOUNCEMENT.

OUR INTEL SUGGESTS THAT GLOBAL CLIMATE CHANGE IS THE WORK OF--

--ISIS!!

OR ISIL, OR WHATEVER IT IS WE'RE CALLING THEM THIS WEEK.

THE PUBLIC REACTS WITH ALARM.

I DIDN'T REALIZE *TERRORISTS* WERE BEHIND GLOBAL WARMING! THIS CHANGES *EVERYTHING*!

WE MUST DO WHATEVER IT *TAKES* TO ELIMINATE THIS THREAT TO THE HOMELAND!

SOME WONDER IF IT'S ALREADY TOO LATE.

RISING SEA LEVELS AND EXTREME WEATHER WILL DO MORE HARM TO AMERICAN CITIES THAN BIN LADEN COULD EVER HAVE *IMAGINED*!

THESE CLIMATE TERRORISTS ARE *TRULY* DIABOLICAL!

BUT AMERICANS RISE TO THE CHALLENGE WITH PATRIOTIC RESOLVE.

WE'LL DEFEAT THOSE TERRORIST SUMBITCHES--

--BY *REDUCING* OUR CARBON *EMISSIONS*!

U.S.A! U.S.A!

THOUGH OF COURSE CIVIL LIBERTIES ARE TRAMPLED IN THE PROCESS.

THE KOCH BROTHERS MAY BE CLIMATE DENIERS--BUT THEY'RE STILL *AMERICAN CITIZENS*! DO THEY *REALLY* BELONG IN GUANTANAMO?

LISTEN, PAL--THEY GAVE UP *THEIR* RIGHTS WHEN THEY DECLARED *CLIMATE WAR* ON THE *UNITED STATES* OF *AMERICA*!

AND *THEN*--

OUR INTEL SUGGESTS THAT AMERICA'S CRUMBLING INFRASTRUCTURE IS THE WORK OF--

--ISIS!!

SO IF WE DON'T REPAIR OUR ROADS AND BRIDGES--

THE *TER-RORISTS* HAVE *WON*!

TOM TOMORROW ©2014

THIS MODERN WORLD

by TOM TOMORROW

CITIZENS

WE'RE IN A SEMI-DECLARED SORTA KINDA NOT QUITE **WAR THING**

ARE YOU DOING YOUR PART?

#HASHTAGS ARE WEAPONS OF WAR

#GET TRENDING!

VIRAL VIDEOS FOR VICTORY!

Dump something unpleasant on your head TODAY!

We're all in this TOGETHER

Have you changed YOUR avatar yet?

You never know who's listening

Please speak clearly so we can hear you

I WANT YOU

TO "LIKE" ENDLESS WAR

TOM TOMORROW ©2014

THIS MODERN WORLD

by TOM TOMORROW

THE COUNTER-INTUITIVIST

OIL SPILLS...ARE **GOOD** FOR THE ENVIRONMENT!

HE'S **SO** FASCINATING!

YOU NEVER KNOW **WHAT** HE'LL SAY NEXT!

HIS OUTSIDE-THE-BOX IDEAS WILL **DAZZLE** YOU!

DAMMIT! I'VE GOT A FLAT **TIRE**!

WHY NOT SCRAP THE ENTIRE **CAR**? IT **COULD** BE THE MOST ECONOMICALLY SENSIBLE COURSE OF ACTION!

WHATEVER **YOU** THINK--**HE** THINKS SOMETHING MORE INTERESTING!

RESTRICTING ABORTION... **INCREASES** ABORTION RIGHTS!

THE BEST WAY TO CONTROL GUNS...IS TO **NOT** CONTROL GUNS!

HIS INTELLECTUAL AGILITY **CON-FOUNDS** LESSER MINDS!

IF YOU WANT TO REGULATE WALL STREET...YOU MUST **ELIMINATE** REGULATIONS!

THAT MAKES NO SENSE.

CAN'T KEEP UP, EH? YOUR LOSS, TINY BRAIN!

YES, HE KNOWS WHAT IT TAKES TO STAND OUT FROM THE CROWD IN **THIS** MODERN WORLD!

CONTRARY TO WHAT YOU MAY HAVE HEARD--

--CUTE KITTENS...ARE ACTUALLY NOT CUTE AT **ALL**!

CONSIDER **MY** MIND BLOWN.

BUT CAN HE WITHSTAND THE CHALLENGE OF THE **COUNTER**-COUNTER-INTUITIVIST?

IRAQ WAS THIS NATION'S GREATEST FOREIGN POLICY SUCCESS!

IF YOU DISCOUNT THE TRIUMPH OF **VIETNAM**!

GASP! HIS CON-TRARIANISM... STRONGER THAN MINE...

MUSN'T... GIVE UP...

...UNLESS IT WOULD BE THE MOST COUNTER-INTUITIVE THING TO DO!

TOM TOMORROW ©2014

41

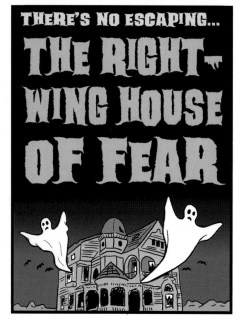

THIS MODERN WORLD
by TOM TOMORROW

THERE'S NO ESCAPING...

THE RIGHT-WING HOUSE OF FEAR

CAN YOU ENDURE THE TERRIFYING CACOPHONY OF *EBOLA HYSTERIA*?

WHYYYYYY HASN'T OBAMA *DONE SOMETHING*??

EVERYONE'S GOING TO *DIIIEEEEE*!!

WILL YOU BE DRIVEN TO *MADNESS* BY THE SPECTER OF ISIS FIGHTERS COMING TO *GET YOU*?

THEY MIGHT BE HIDING UNDER *YOOOUUUR BED*!!

OR IN THE *CLOSET*!!

CAN YOUR TRADITIONAL VALUES *POSSIBLY* WITHSTAND THE CREEPING MENACE OF *GAY MARRIAGE*?

IT'S *LEEEGAL* IN MANY STATES!!

DITCH THE WIFE! RUN OFF WITH A *DUUUUDE*!!

YOU KNOW YOU *WAANNNT* TO!!

DARE YOU FACE THE UNIMAGINABLE TERROR OF *WOMEN'S REPRODUCTIVE FREEDOM*?

THEY CONTROL THEIR *OOWWWNN* BODIES!

THEY CAN HAVE SEX WITH WHOMEVER THEY *CHOOOOSE*!

AND IT MIGHT NOT BE *YOUUU*!

NOT TO MENTION THE FEARSOME HORRORS OF REFUGEE CHILDREN AT THE *BORDER*--SCIENTISTS WHO BELIEVE IN *GLOBAL WARMING*-- MINORITIES IN *GENERAL*--

--AND *SOOOO* MUCH *MORRRE*!

DON'T LET THEM *GET* US!

I THINK I JUST WET MY *PANTS*!

BE *AFRAAIIID*...BE *VERRRRYYY AFRAAAIIID*...

THIS MODERN WORLD

by TOM TOMORROW

OTHER DANGEROUS EPIDEMICS IN AMERICA

GUNFLUENZA

THE MORE PEOPLE THERE ARE WAVING **GUNS** AROUND--THE **SAFER** EVERYONE WILL BE!

MAKES PERFECT SENSE TO **ME!**

CLIMATE DENIAL FEVER

GLOBAL WARMING IS A **HOAX** PERPETRATED BY GREEDY GRANT-SEEKING **SCIENTISTS!**

FORTUNATELY, THE ALTRUISTIC **KOCH BROTHERS** ARE **ONTO** THEIR NEFARIOUS SCHEME!

SEVERE ACUTE INEQUALITY SYNDROME

I'M NOT ONE OF THE RICHEST ONE PERCENT WHO OWN MORE WEALTH THAN THE BOTTOM NINETY PERCENT **COMBINED**--

--BUT MAYBE SOMEDAY I **WILL** BE-- AND I WOULDN'T WANT TO FACE A BURDENSOME TAX RATE **THEN!**

ONLINE MISOGYNITIS

THIS STUPID FEMALE WROTE A STUPID THING ON THE **INTERNET**--

--SO WE'RE INUNDATING HER WITH ANONYMOUS RAPE AND DEATH THREATS.

ALL IN THE SPIRIT OF OPEN DISCOURSE AND ETHICAL DEBATE!

RIGHT-WING BRAIN ROT

THE **REAL** THREAT TO AMERICA IS DARK-SKINNED, EBOLA-INFECTED **TERROR CHILDREN** SNEAKING ACROSS THE BORDER TO **KILL US ALL!**

AND HIGH TAXES ON THE RICH.

TOM TOMORROW ©2014

43

THIS MODERN WORLD

by TOM TOMORROW

I DON'T **CARE** WHAT THOSE WHINING HEALTH CARE WORKERS SAY--WE NEED A MANDATORY QUARANTINE FOR ANYONE WHO'S BEEN ANYWHERE **NEAR** AN EBOLA OUTBREAK!

OR BETTER YET A BAN ON TRAVEL FROM THOSE COUNTRIES **ENTIRELY!** AND FROM COUNTRIES **NEAR** THOSE COUNTRIES, JUST TO BE **SAFE!**

WE CAN'T TAKE **ANY** CHANCES! WHEN YOU'RE DEALING WITH A DISEASE THAT COULD POTENTIALLY KILL THOUSANDS OF AMERICANS--

--YOU HAVE TO TAKE EVERY POSSIBLE PRECAUTION TO KEEP IT FROM **SPREADING**--NO MATTER THE INCONVENIENCE! IT'S **EVERYONE'S** RESPONSIBILITY!

NO EXCEPTIONS!

ON AN ENTIRELY UNRELATED NOTE, HAVE YOU GOTTEN A FLU SHOT YET?

NO, IT'S SUCH A HASSLE.

WHY?

TOM TOMORROW ©2014

THIS MODERN WORLD

by TOM TOMORROW

IN THE FINAL DAYS OF THE MOST EXPENSIVE MIDTERM IN HISTORY, REPUBLICANS MADE THEIR BEST CASE TO AMERICAN VOTERS.

ISIS!

OBAMA!

EBOLA!

EEK!

WHAT THEIR SUBSEQUENT VICTORY **MEANT** IS OPEN TO INTERPRETATION.

THE PEOPLE SENT A **MESSAGE**--

--THAT THEY WANT THE 2.3% EXCISE TAX ON MEDICAL DEVICES REPEALED.*

YEAH!!

WAIT, WHAT?

*THIS ACTUALLY IS ONE OF HIS TOP PRIORITIES.

BUT A NEW ERA OF LEADERSHIP IS CLEARLY AT HAND.

THE HEARING ON WHETHER GLOBAL WARMING IS A **HOAX** OR A **FRAUD** WILL NOW COME TO ORDER.

OUR FIRST ORDER OF BUSINESS-- **BENGHAZI!**

INHOFE

MEANWHILE DEMOCRATIC STRATEGISTS WILL TRY TO FIGURE OUT WHAT WENT WRONG.

SO IF PEOPLE VOTED **FOR** LIBERAL POLICIES--BUT AGAINST OUR **CANDIDATES**--

--THEN CLEARLY WE MUST MOVE **FURTHER** TO THE **RIGHT!**

I SEE NO OTHER POSSIBLE CONCLUSION!

AND THE PRESIDENT MUST CHOOSE BETWEEN STANDING FIRM AND FINDING COMMON GROUND.

STAY STRONG! USE YOUR **VETO!**

IGNORE **HIM!** DON'T YOU WANT TO "WORK TOGETHER" TO "GET THINGS DONE"?

THOUGH IT'S REALLY TIME TO LOOK FORWARD AND NOT BACKWARD.

THE 2016 ELECTION IS ONLY **SEVEN HUNDRED AND THIRTY DAYS AWAY!**

AND THE RACE BETWEEN HILLARY CLINTON AND **UN-NAMED REPUBLICAN OPPONENT** IS **REALLY** HEATING UP!

WE'LL HAVE THE LATEST NUMBERS AFTER THESE MESSAGES!

Action McNews Network

TOM TOMORROW ©2014

THIS MODERN WORLD

by TOM TOMORROW

THIS MODERN WORLD

by TOM TOMORROW

In the awesome world of... THE FUTURE

WE'LL CARRY INDIVIDUAL COMMUNICATION AND TRACKING DEVICES WITH US AT **ALL TIMES!**

PERSONAL PRIVACY IS **SO** TWENTIETH CENTURY!

THESE DEVICES WILL ALLOW US TO SUMMON A RIDE FROM AN UNREGULATED INDEPENDENT CONTRACTOR--ANY TIME WE **WANT!**

OUR PRIMITIVE ANCESTORS COULD NEVER HAVE **DREAMED** OF SUCH ADVANCED TECHNOLOGY!

THE FUTURE'S SO BRIGHT, I GOTTA WEAR INTERACTIVE **SUNGLASSES!**

SUCH SERVICES WILL BE MADE POSSIBLE BY DISRUPTIVE THINKERS, WHO WILL INCIDENTALLY COLLECT AS MUCH **DATA** AS **POSSIBLE!**

THIS IS OUR NOT-AT-ALL CREEPY OVERVIEW OF **UBER** RIDERS WHO RECENTLY HAD **ONE NIGHT STANDS!**

WE CALL IT OUR "**RIDES OF GLORY**" MAP!*

DEPT. OF NOT-AT-ALL CREEPY DATA ANALYTICS

UBER

*A REAL THING.

AND YOU'D BETTER BELIEVE THESE FUTURE ENTREPRENEURS WILL HAVE INNOVATIVE IDEAS FOR DEALING WITH THEIR **CRITICS!**

WHAT IF WE SPENT A MILLION **FUTURE DOLLARS** TO DIG UP DIRT ON ANY JOURNALIST WHO DARES TO **QUESTION** US?

IMAGINE HOW DISRUPTIVE **THAT** WOULD BE!

IS HE OUTSIDE THE BOX OR **WHAT?**

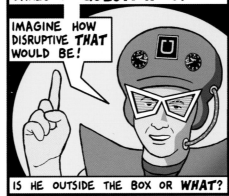

COMING UP **NEXT** TIME: HOW TECHNOLOGY WILL GIVE US ACCESS TO THE INNERMOST THOUGHTS AND DESIRES OF **MILLIONS** OF **RANDOM STRANGERS!**

SURELY THE "**INTER-NET**" WILL USHER IN AN UNHERALDED AGE OF COMPASSION AND UNDERSTANDING!

WHAT COULD POSSIBLY GO **WRONG?**

IT'S ALL WAITING--IN **THE FUTURE!**

TOM TOMORROW©2014

THIS MODERN WORLD

by TOM TOMORROW

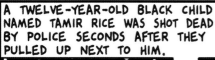

Panel 1: MICHAEL BROWN WAS SHOT DEAD IN THE STREET BY OFFICER DARREN WILSON.

YES, BUT HE HAD JUST *SHOPLIFTED*!

Panel 2: A BLACK MAN NAMED ERIC GARNER WAS CHOKED TO DEATH BY NEW YORK CITY POLICE.

YES, BUT HE WAS SELLING *UNTAXED CIGARETTES*!

Panel 3: A BLACK MAN NAMED JOHN CRAWFORD WAS SHOT DEAD BY POLICE IN AN OHIO WALMART.

YES, BUT HE WAS *HOLDING A BB GUN*!

Panel 4: A TWELVE-YEAR-OLD BLACK CHILD NAMED TAMIR RICE WAS SHOT DEAD BY POLICE SECONDS AFTER THEY PULLED UP NEXT TO HIM.

YES, BUT HE HAD A *TOY GUN*! *AND* HIS FATHER HAS A HISTORY OF DOMESTIC *ABUSE*!

Panel 6: I HEARD THAT A WHITE GUY OPENLY CARRYING A LOADED AK-47 WAS BRIEFLY QUESTIONED BY POLICE, AND THEN SENT ON HIS WAY.

WHAT?! THAT'S AN *OUTRAGE*! WHAT PART OF *CONSTITUTIONAL RIGHTS* DO THESE FASCISTS NOT *UNDERSTAND*?!

AN INJURY TO *ONE* IS AN INJURY TO *ALL*!

I DON'T KNOW HOW YOU BEAR THE PAIN.

THIS MODERN WORLD

by TOM TOMORROW

RIGHT-WING LESSONS LEARNED

1. IT'S NEVER ABOUT RACE.

IT'S ABOUT "THUGS" IN "BAGGY PANTS" WHO LISTEN TO "*RAP*"!

I DON'T EVEN *SEE* COLOR!

LITERALLY, I'M COLORBLIND.

2. IT'S UNFAIR TO HOLD POLICE ACCOUNTABLE FOR THEIR ACTIONS.

MUST THEY BE PESTERED WITH ANNOYING QUESTIONS EVERY TIME THEY *KILL* SOMEONE?

HOW CAN THEY EVEN *FUNCTION* UNDER SUCH CONDITIONS?

3. VICTIMS CAN BE DISREGARDED IF THEY WERE IMPERFECT HUMAN BEINGS.

MIKE BROWN WAS A *SHOPLIFTER* WHO LOOKED *MENACING*! AND ERIC GARNER WAS *OBESE*!

END OF *DISCUSSION*!

4. A GRAND JURY DECISION = AN UNEQUIVOCAL EXONERATION.

WHAT DO PEOPLE *WANT*--SOME SORT OF NON-SECRET, ADVERSARIAL SYSTEM OF JUSTICE BALANCING DEFENSE *AND* PROSECUTION?

HOW ABOUT FREE *PONIES* WHILE WE'RE *AT* IT?

5. PROTESTERS ARE AN IRRATIONAL BUNCH.

IN MY OPINION AS A PROFESSIONAL SERIOUS PERSON, THEY'RE ALL COMPLETELY *BONKERS*!

THANK YOU FOR THAT *EXPERT ANALYSIS*!

Action McNews Network

6. BLACK LEADERS ALWAYS HAVE ULTERIOR MOTIVES.

THOSE "RACE HUSTLERS" JUST WANT TO EXPLOIT RACIAL TENSION FOR THEIR OWN GAIN!

WHICH IS WEIRD SINCE NONE OF THIS IS *ABOUT* RACE!

7. IF MARTIN LUTHER KING WERE ALIVE TODAY HE'D BE A WHITE CONSERVATIVE.

WHY CAN'T *TODAY'S* BLACK AMERICANS LIVE UP TO OUR SELECTIVELY-EDITED VERSION OF HIM?

THAT ONE QUOTE OF HIS IS *VERY* INSPIRING!

8. WHITE PEOPLE ARE THE REAL VICTIMS.

I JUST FEEL LIKE THERE MIGHT BE *SOME* RACISM LEFT IN SOCIETY.

THAT'S BECAUSE YOU'RE THE *REAL* RACIST!

DR. KING WOULD BE *SO* DISAPPOINTED!

TOM TOMORROW ©2014

THIS MODERN WORLD

by TOM TOMORROW

2014 IN REVIEW

A HIGHLY SUBJECTIVE AND ASSUREDLY INCOMPLETE LOOK BACK AT THE YEAR THAT WAS

PART THE FIRST

JAN. 2: DAVID BROOKS ACKNOWLEDGES SMOKING WEED IN HIS YOUTH; INSISTS IT SHOULD REMAIN ILLEGAL.

I'M HIGH ON UPPER CLASS PRIVILEGE!

JAN. 9: MASSIVE CHEMICAL SPILL LEAVES 300,000 WEST VIRGINIANS WITHOUT WATER; AMERICANS SHRUG.

WELL IT'S NOT LIKE **TERRORISTS** DID IT!

JAN. 23: OXFAM REPORT NOTES THAT 85 RICHEST PEOPLE OWN AS MUCH AS BOTTOM HALF OF THE PLANET COMBINED.

THEY ARE **ACHIEVERS!**

WHY DO LIBTARDS WANT TO PUNISH **SUCCESS**?

JAN. 24: BILLIONAIRE INVESTOR COMPARES CRITICISM OF RICH TO THE HOLOCAUST.

YOU KNOW WHO **ELSE** MADE SNARKY COMMENTS ABOUT PEOPLE?

WHO?

FEB. 20: FLORIDA JUDGE ORDERS GUNS RETURNED TO BLIND MAN ACQUITTED OF KILLING FRIEND UNDER "STAND YOUR GROUND" STATUTE.

WE COULD ADD SOMETHING, BUT REALLY, WHAT WOULD BE THE POINT?

FEB. 25: LORD OF DARKNESS AND ALL THAT IS VILE DICK CHENEY SURFACES TO DECLARE--

"(OBAMA) WOULD RATHER SPEND THE MONEY ON **FOOD STAMPS** THAN...ON A STRONG MILITARY OR SUPPORT FOR OUR TROOPS!"

FEB. 26: RAND PAUL BLOCKS APPOINTMENT OF SURGEON GENERAL WHO SAYS GUN VIOLENCE IS A HEALTH ISSUE.

YOU'LL PRY HIS NOMINATION FROM MY **COLD DEAD FINGERS!**

FEB. 27: GUARDIAN REVEALS BRITISH GCHQ INTERCEPTED MILLIONS OF WEBCAM IMAGES.

OH WELL! I HAVE NOTHING TO HIDE!

MARCH: DISAPPEARANCE OF FLIGHT 370 LEADS TO VERY INFORMATIVE CABLE NEWS SPECULATION.

WAS IT SUCKED INTO A **BLACK HOLE**?

I BET THAT COULD TOTALLY HAPPEN.

MARCH 4: LINDSAY GRAHAM BLAMES RUSSIAN INVASION OF UKRAINE ON...**BENGHAZI!**

"WHEN YOU KILL AMERICANS AND NOBODY PAYS A PRICE, YOU **INVITE** THIS TYPE OF AGGRESSION!"

MARCH 19: BILL "ARMCHAIR WARRIOR" KRISTOL CHASTISES AMERICANS FOR THEIR INEXPLICABLE RELUCTANCE TO START MORE WARS.

WHAT ARE YA--A BUNCH OF **WIMPS**?

APRIL 3: DEADBEAT RANCHER BECOMES OVERNIGHT FOLK HERO TO CONSERVATIVES.

APRIL 24: DEADBEAT RANCHER SHARES HIS THOUGHTS ON "THE NEGRO," IS DROPPED BY CONSERVATIVES LIKE A HOT POTATO.

MAY 27: JOHN KERRY CALLS EDWARD SNOWDEN A "COWARD" AND "TRAITOR" WHO SHOULD "MAN UP--COME BACK TO THE U.S!"

AND THEN WE'LL THROW HIM IN A HOLE SO DEEP, HE'LL NEVER SEE DAYLIGHT AGAIN.

MAY 27: IN WAKE OF ELLIOT RODGER SHOOTING SPREE, FORGOTTEN RIGHT WING ICON JOE THE PLUMBER MAKES BID FOR MORE ATTENTION.

"YOUR DEAD KIDS DON'T TRUMP **MY** CONSTITUTIONAL RIGHTS!"

JUNE 30: SUPREME COURT AFFIRMS THAT CORPORATIONS ARE RELIGIOUS PEOPLE.

THE SEX-HAVING FLESH PEOPLE OFFEND **MY** SINCERELY HELD BELIEFS!

HOBBY LOBBY

CONTINUED NEXT WEEK!

TOM TOMORROW ©2014

THIS MODERN WORLD
by TOM TOMORROW

2014 IN REVIEW

A HIGHLY SUBJECTIVE AND ASSUREDLY INCOMPLETE LOOK BACK AT THE YEAR THAT WAS

PART THE SECOND

JULY 19: ANTI-IMMIGRANT ACTIVISTS START CAMPAIGN TO MAIL DIRTY UNDERWEAR TO REFUGEE CHILDREN IN U.S. DETAINMENT.

BECAUSE WE ARE TERRIBLE HUMAN BEINGS!

SIMPLY AWFUL!

JULY 29: URBAN INSTITUTE REPORTS ONE IN THREE AMERICANS ARE BEING CHASED BY DEBT COLLECTORS.

THIS IS A **TOTALLY** SUSTAINABLE SYSTEM!

JULY 17: R.I.P. ERIC GARNER, CHOKED TO DEATH BY NYC POLICE.

AUG. 5: R.I.P. JOHN CRAWFORD, SHOT BY OHIO POLICE WHILE CARRYING TOY GUN IN WALMART.

AUG. 9: R.I.P. MICHAEL BROWN, SHOT DEAD BY OFFICER DARREN WILSON.

R.I.P. TAMIR RICE AND SO MANY OTHERS.

AUG. 10: FERGUSON POLICE TREAT PROTESTERS WITH DIGNITY AND RESPECT.

MAKE MY DAY, PUNKS.

IN SOME ALTERNATE UNIVERSE MAYBE.

AUG. 21: DARK LORD CHENEY WARNS--

"WHEN YOU SEE (ISIS) BEHEAD AN AMERICAN REPORTER...MAGNIFY THAT A **MILLION TIMES OVER!**"

FOX VIEWERS TREMBLE IN FEAR.

SEPT. 15: LINDSAY "PEARL-CLUTCHING" GRAHAM IS VERY WORRIED ABOUT ISIS.

"THIS PRESIDENT NEEDS TO RISE TO THE OCCASION--"

"--BEFORE WE ALL GET **KILLED** BACK HERE AT HOME!"

SEPT. 18: STARBUCKS BANS GUNS, PLACING GUN OWNERS IN IMAGINARY DANGER.

HOW CAN I FEEL **SAFE** ORDERING A DOUBLE CHOCOLATY CHIP FRAPPUCCINO WITH WHIPPED CREAM--

--WITHOUT A **WEAPON** AT MY SIDE?

SEPT. 30: FIRST U.S. EBOLA CASE SETS OFF EPIDEMIC OF MEDIA PANIC.

THIS JUST IN--**EVERYONE'S GOING TO DIE!**

JUST NOT NECESSARILY NOW. OR FROM EBOLA.

MONTH OF OCTOBER: "GAMERGATERS" EXPRESS THEIR CONCERN FOR ETHICS IN GAMING JOURNALISM BY SENDING RAPE AND DEATH THREATS TO WOMEN.

IT'S THE CIVIL RIGHTS STRUGGLE OF OUR ERA!

OCT. 22: HOMELAND SECURITY IS ON THE CASE-- CONFISCATING BOOTLEG K.C. ROYALS PANTIES FROM SMALL SHOPKEEPER.

COPYRIGHT VIOLATION, MA'AM.

VERY IMPORTANT NATIONAL SECURITY BUSINESS.

NOV 4: LOWEST VOTER TURNOUT IN 75 YEARS.

ISN'T VOTER APATHY DREADFUL TO BEHOLD?

TRULY A DISGRACE.

NOV. 21: REPORT FROM GOP-CONTROLLED COMMITTEE FINDS "NO WRONGDOING" IN BENGHAZI; GOP LEADERSHIP DOUBLES DOWN ON FURTHER INVESTIGATIONS.

MAYBE WE'LL GET THE ANSWER WE WANT THE **EIGHTH** TIME WE TRY!

DEC. 9: DARK LORD CHENEY BLASTS TORTURE REPORT.

WE SUBJECTED DETAINEES TO UNSPEAKABLE BRUTALITY AND SEXUAL ABUSE--

--IN ORDER TO PRESERVE OUR **CORE AMERICAN VALUES!**

DEC. 17: CUBA OPENS NORMALIZATION TALKS WITH COUNTRY NOTORIOUS FOR TORTURE AND SURVEILLANCE.

WE HOPE WE CAN BE A POSITIVE INFLUENCE.

REST OF '14: WAY TOO MUCH MORE OF THE SAME.

HAPPY WAR ON CHRISTMAS, EVERYONE!

ALSO NEW YEAR'S!

NEXT YEAR: EVEN **MORE!**

TOM TOMORROW ©2014

THIS MODERN WORLD

by TOM TOMORROW

THE ADMINISTRATION DID ITS BEST TO PROTECT THE COUNTRY FROM THE UNPLEASANTNESS OF THE TORTURE REPORT.

SORRY SIR--I *TRIED* TO STALL THE RELEASE, BUT NO LUCK.

WHAT PART OF "LOOKING FORWARD, NOT BACKWARD" DO PEOPLE FAIL TO COM-*PREHEND*?

BUT A 500-PAGE SUMMARY* WAS FINALLY MADE PUBLIC--REMINDING AMERICANS OF THINGS THEY HAD CHOSEN TO FORGET.

APPARENTLY THE CIA WATERBOARDED DETAINEES--CHAINED THEM IN STRESS POSITIONS--AND DID ALL *SORTS* OF TERRIBLE THINGS!

YOU KNOW, THAT DOES SOUND VAGUELY FAMILIAR, NOW THAT YOU MENTION IT.

*THE FULL 6000-PAGE REPORT REMAINS CLASSIFIED.

SOME TRIED TO PUT A POSITIVE SPIN ON IT ALL.

DOESN'T OUR **ACKNOWLEDGMENT** OF THE GROTESQUE AND SAVAGE ACTS COMMITTED BY OUR GOVERNMENT IN SECRET TORTURE DUNGEONS--

--PROVE OUR FUNDAMENTAL *DECENCY*?

IT'S AMERICAN EXCEPTIONALISM FOR THE *WIN*!

TORTURE APOLOGISTS DUSTED OFF *THEIR* FAVORITE TALKING POINTS--

WE *DIDN'T* TORTURE ANYONE--

--BUT IF WE DID IT WAS LEGAL--

--AND TOTALLY NECESSARY--

--AND *COMPLETELY* DEFENSIBLE--

--BUT IF YOU DON'T STOP TALKING ABOUT IT THE TERRORISTS WILL ATTACK AND KILL US ALL--

--AND IT'LL BE YOUR FAULT.

--AND ARGUED THAT THE TORTURERS ACTUALLY DESERVE *THANKS* FOR THEIR SERVICE.

WELL, TIME TO GO *RECTALLY FEED* THE PRISONER!

WHILE WE THREATEN TO *RAPE HIS MOTHER*!

GOD BLESS YOU MEN-- AND GOD BLESS *AMERICA*!

MEANWHILE, LORD OF DARKNESS AND ALL THAT IS VILE *DICK CHENEY* REALLY DIDN'T SEE WHAT ALL THE *FUSS* WAS ABOUT.

SO IT SAYS WE USED FALSE INFORMATION OBTAINED THROUGH TORTURE TO JUSTIFY THE WAR WE WANTED IN *IRAQ*?

WELL, I THINK THE LESSON IS *CLEAR*--

--TORTURE *WORKS*.

HARUMPH.

TOM TOMORROW ©2014

THIS MODERN WORLD

by TOM TOMORROW

1. SEVERAL UNARMED BLACK MEN, AND ONE CHILD, ARE KILLED BY POLICE IN SHORT SUCCESSION.

I

CAN'T

BREATHE

2. A MASSIVE PROTEST MOVEMENT EMERGES.

HANDS UP

BLACK LIVES MATTER

3. POLITICIANS ACKNOWLEDGE THAT PROBLEMS EXIST.

"A DEEP DISTRUST EXISTS BETWEEN LAW ENFORCEMENT AND COMMUNITIES OF COLOR."

"I HAVE HAD TO TALK TO DANTE FOR YEARS ABOUT...HOW TO TAKE SPECIAL CARE IN ANY ENCOUNTER HE HAS WITH THE POLICE."

4. LUNATIC KILLS TWO OFFICERS; POLITICIANS WHO ACKNOWLEDGED EXISTENCE OF PROBLEMS ARE BLAMED.

MAYOR DE BLASIO HAS **BLOOD ON HIS HANDS** FOR HIS MILD CRITICISM OF POLICE TACTICS!

WHY DOES OBAMA **HATE ALL COPS**?

5. NYPD THROWS TEMPER TANTRUM.

OFFICER BABY NOT **LIKE** YOU!

YOU MAKE OFFICER BABY **MAD**!

?

CONCLUSION: POLICE MUST ALWAYS RECEIVE UNQUESTIONING DEFERENCE, AND NEVER, EVER BE HELD ACCOUNTABLE FOR THEIR ACTIONS.

UM--I'M NOT SURE THAT'S **REALLY** THE CONCLUSION--

ALSO WE HAVE GUNS. AND TASERS. AND WE'RE **PISSED**.

UH--YES **SIR**!

WHATEVER YOU SAY.

SIR.

POLICE

TOM TOMORROW ©2015

THIS MODERN WORLD

by TOM TOMORROW

FIVE CARTOONISTS AND SEVEN OTHERS* ARE KILLED BY GUNMEN AT THE OFFICES OF A SATIRICAL NEWSPAPER.

AND THEN--THE *HOT TAKES* BEGIN! THIS PROVES THE NEED FOR *MORE* SURVEILLANCE AND TORTURE!

EVERY MUSLIM MUST TWEET A DENUNCIATION OF THE ATTACK OR ELSE IT MEANS THE ENTIRE RELIGION *SUPPORTS* IT!

*R.I.P. (PICTURED): STÉPHANE CHARBONNIER, JEAN CABUT, GEORGES WOLINSKI, BERNARD VERLHAC, PHILIPPE HONORÉ, BERNARD MARIS, MICHEL RENAUD, AND FRENCH MUSLIM POLICE OFFICER AHMED MERABET...(NOT PICTURED): MUSTAPHA OURRAD, ELSA CAYAT, FREDERIC BOISSEAU AND FRANCK BRINSOLARO.

SATIRE IS NOT A CAPITAL OFFENSE, EVEN WHEN IT'S OFFENSIVE.

IF EVERYONE IN PARIS WAS CARRYING A *GUN* THIS NEVER WOULD HAVE HAPPENED!

SURE, MASSACRES ARE BAD--

--BUT WEREN'T THEY KIND OF *ASKING* FOR IT?

BONUS FUN FACT: ALL THOSE CARTOONS YOU'VE SEEN WITH THE GIANT PENS AND PENCILS ARE *NOT* VISUAL METAPHORS FOR THE POWER OF SATIRE--BUT RATHER, *LITERAL REPRESENTATIONS* OF STANDARD CARTOONING TOOLS!

TOM TOMORROW ©2015

THIS MODERN WORLD

by TOM TOMORROW

CHARLIE HEBD'OVERLOAD
NOTES FROM THE WEEK THAT WAS

AFTER "JE SUIS CHARLIE" CAME THE INEVITABLE SOCIAL MEDIA **BACKLASH.**

MASSACRES ARE AN OFFENSE TO **DECENCY**, OF COURSE--

--BUT SO WERE THOSE UNPLEASANT **CARTOONS!**

THE WORK **WAS** OFTEN CRUDE, AND DELIBERATELY PROVOCATIVE--

--BUT SATIRE IS ALSO PRONE TO MISINTERPRETATION--ESPECIALLY IF YOU DON'T SPEAK THE LANGUAGE OR UNDERSTAND THE CONTEXT--

ARE YOU DONE **CARTOONSPLAINING?**

PROBABLY NOT.

ANYWAY, YOU CAN ALWAYS COUNT ON THE INTERNET TO LET YOU KNOW THAT VICTIMS HAD IMPERFECTIONS!

SHE WAS WEARING A **SHORT SKIRT!**

HE LOOKED LIKE A MENACING **THUG!**

THEY DREW THINGS THAT MADE PEOPLE **MAD!**

MEANWHILE, WORLD LEADERS AND DIPLOMATS MARCHED IN SUPPORT OF **FREEDOM OF EXPRESSION**... INCLUDING THE AMBASSADOR FROM **SAUDI ARABIA**--

--WHERE **RAIF BADAWI** WAS JUST SENTENCED TO 10 YEARS AND 1,000 LASHES (50 A WEEK FOR 20 WEEKS)--FOR **BLOGGING.**

FRANCE ITSELF FOLLOWED UP BY ARRESTING DOZENS OF PEOPLE FOR HATE SPEECH, INCLUDING A CONTROVERSIAL **COMEDIAN.**

NOUS, ON **AIME** LA SATIRE! C'EST JUSTE **L'IRONIE** QUI NE NOUS EST PAS TRÈS CLAIRE!*

PRES. HOLLANDE

*WE **LOVE** SATIRE! WE'RE JUST NOT VERY CLEAR ON **IRONY!**

FINALLY: MAYBE WE CAN STOP WITH THE BIG PENCIL CARTOONS NOW?

HEY TERRORIST DUDE--I REPRESENT THE **INDOMITABLE SPIRIT** OF **SATIRE**--AND I'M HERE TO **RUB YOU OUT!**

OH **NO!** NOT A GIANT PENCIL SYMBOLIZING **SATIRE!!**

SATIRE

TOM TOMORROW ©2015

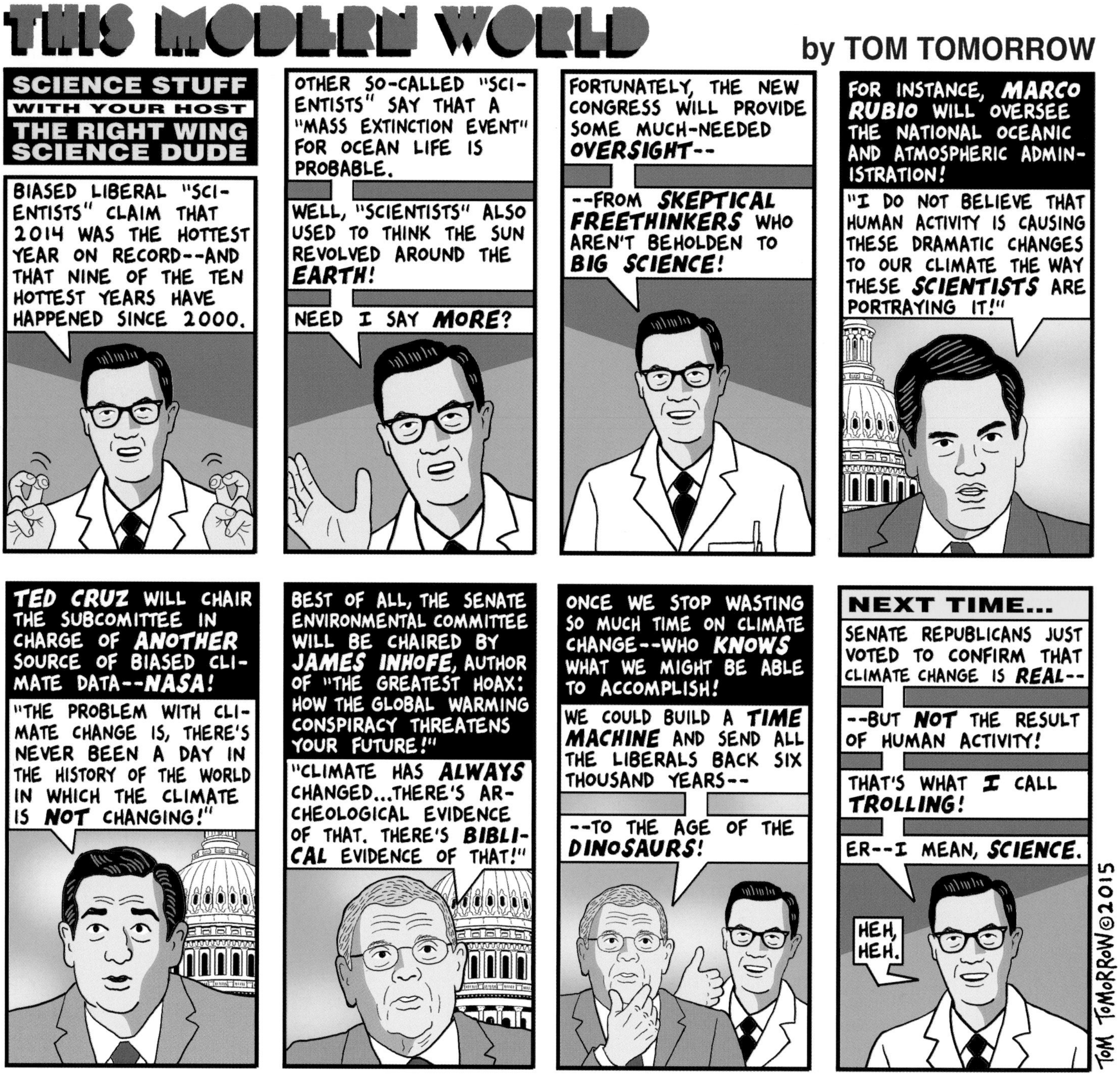
THIS MODERN WORLD
by TOM TOMORROW
SCIENCE STUFF
WITH YOUR HOST
THE RIGHT WING SCIENCE DUDE
BIASED LIBERAL "SCIENTISTS" CLAIM THAT 2014 WAS THE HOTTEST YEAR ON RECORD--AND THAT NINE OF THE TEN HOTTEST YEARS HAVE HAPPENED SINCE 2000.
OTHER SO-CALLED "SCIENTISTS" SAY THAT A "MASS EXTINCTION EVENT" FOR OCEAN LIFE IS PROBABLE.
WELL, "SCIENTISTS" ALSO USED TO THINK THE SUN REVOLVED AROUND THE EARTH!
NEED I SAY MORE?
FORTUNATELY, THE NEW CONGRESS WILL PROVIDE SOME MUCH-NEEDED OVERSIGHT--
--FROM SKEPTICAL FREETHINKERS WHO AREN'T BEHOLDEN TO BIG SCIENCE!
FOR INSTANCE, MARCO RUBIO WILL OVERSEE THE NATIONAL OCEANIC AND ATMOSPHERIC ADMINISTRATION!
"I DO NOT BELIEVE THAT HUMAN ACTIVITY IS CAUSING THESE DRAMATIC CHANGES TO OUR CLIMATE THE WAY THESE SCIENTISTS ARE PORTRAYING IT!"
TED CRUZ WILL CHAIR THE SUBCOMITTEE IN CHARGE OF ANOTHER SOURCE OF BIASED CLIMATE DATA--NASA!
"THE PROBLEM WITH CLIMATE CHANGE IS, THERE'S NEVER BEEN A DAY IN THE HISTORY OF THE WORLD IN WHICH THE CLIMATE IS NOT CHANGING!"
BEST OF ALL, THE SENATE ENVIRONMENTAL COMMITTEE WILL BE CHAIRED BY JAMES INHOFE, AUTHOR OF "THE GREATEST HOAX: HOW THE GLOBAL WARMING CONSPIRACY THREATENS YOUR FUTURE!"
"CLIMATE HAS ALWAYS CHANGED...THERE'S ARCHEOLOGICAL EVIDENCE OF THAT. THERE'S BIBLICAL EVIDENCE OF THAT!"
ONCE WE STOP WASTING SO MUCH TIME ON CLIMATE CHANGE--WHO KNOWS WHAT WE MIGHT BE ABLE TO ACCOMPLISH!
WE COULD BUILD A TIME MACHINE AND SEND ALL THE LIBERALS BACK SIX THOUSAND YEARS--
--TO THE AGE OF THE DINOSAURS!
NEXT TIME...
SENATE REPUBLICANS JUST VOTED TO CONFIRM THAT CLIMATE CHANGE IS REAL--
--BUT NOT THE RESULT OF HUMAN ACTIVITY!
THAT'S WHAT I CALL TROLLING!
ER--I MEAN, SCIENCE.
HEH, HEH.
TOM TOMORROW©2015

THIS MODERN WORLD

by TOM TOMORROW

SCIENTISTS SAY THAT 2014 WAS THE HOTTEST YEAR ON *RECORD*.

IF THERE'S SO MUCH GLOBAL WARMING, WHY IS IT SO *COLD* OUT?

BIFF, DIDN'T YOU *HEAR*? SENATE REPUBLICANS JUST VOTED FOR AN AMENDMENT ADMITTING THAT CLIMATE CHANGE IS *REAL*!

IT WAS A LEGISLATIVE MANEUVER TO AVOID ACKNOWLEDGING HUMAN CULPABILITY--BUT INTENTIONALLY OR NOT, THEY'VE OFFICALLY CONCEDED HALF THE *DEBATE*!

THE ONLY THING LEFT TO ARGUE ABOUT NOW IS THE *CAUSE*!

YOU CAN STOP TYING YOURSELF IN PRETZEL KNOTS DENYING THE *OBVIOUS!* YOU NO LONGER HAVE TO LOOK LIKE AN *IDIOT* INSISTING THAT NOTHING'S *WRONG*!

YOU'VE BEEN *LIBERATED*, BIFF! IT'S A *GIFT! EMBRACE* IT!

OR YOU COULD JUST DENY IT EVER HAPPENED.

YOU'LL PRY *MY* AL GORE JOKES FROM MY COLD, DEAD FINGERS.

TOM TOMORROW ©2015

THIS MODERN WORLD

by TOM TOMORROW

Valentine's Day Cards for 2015

My love is highly contagious!

Won't you be my anti-vax Valentine?

MY FEELINGS FOR YOU ARE RAPIDLY WARMING

AND THAT'S NO HOAX!

TO MY ONE TRUE LOVE

BEING WITH YOU IS A REAL BLAST

Valentine, you can fill MY campaign coffers any day!*

*Not a euphemism. Please give me lots of money.

JEB 2016

DEAR VALENTINE, I'VE GOT A TARGET LOCK ON YOU!

(ALONG WITH SEVERAL UN-IDENTIFIED CIVILIANS IN YOUR GENERAL VICINITY)

TOM TOMORROW ©2015

THIS MODERN WORLD

by TOM TOMORROW

--AND THEN THERE WAS THE TIME I STARED **DEATH** IN THE **EYE** ON A CHINOOK HELICOPTER UNDER HEAVY ENEMY FIRE IN **IRAQ**--

UM, SIR--PSST PSST PSST!

INTERESTING! I'VE JUST BEEN INFORMED THAT I SEEM TO HAVE CONFLATED SOMEONE **ELSE'S** EXPERIENCE WITH MY **OWN**!

MEMORY IS CERTAINLY A TRICKY THING!

IT REMINDS ME OF THE TIME I WAS A SECRET AGENT WITH A HEAD FULL OF **IMPLANTED** MEMORIES AND I HAD TO GO TO THE MINING COLONY ON **MARS**--

AHEM! PSST **PSST!**

MY **APOLOGIES**, AMERICA! I SEEM TO HAVE CONFUSED MY OWN LIFE WITH THE PLOT OF THE 1990 VERSION OF "**TOTAL RECALL**"!

AND I DON'T MIND **ADMITTING** WHEN I'VE MADE A MISTAKE!

IT'S THE ONLY WAY NEWS PROFESSIONALS SUCH AS MYSELF CAN MAINTAIN THE **TRUST** OF THE AUDIENCE!

WE HAVE TO REPORT THE TRUTH--AND DAMN THE CONSEQUENCES!

LIKE WHEN WE COURAGEOUSLY EXPOSED THE BUSH ADMINISTRATION'S LIES ABOUT WMD'S IN IRAQ AND SADDAM'S CONNECTIONS TO AL QAEDA!

IT WASN'T **EASY**-- BUT IT WAS THE **RIGHT THING** TO DO!

CAN YOU EVEN **IMAGINE** WHAT KIND OF MESS THE WORLD MIGHT BE IN TODAY IF WE'D SHIRKED OUR DUTY AS JOURNALISTS--

--AND IN-STEAD SERVED AS DE FACTO **PROPAGAN-DISTS**?

SIR! PSST PSST PSST PSST **PSST!**

ER--I MAY HAVE **SLIGHTLY** MIS-REMEMBERED SOME OF THAT.

BUT LET ME TELL YOU ABOUT THE TIME MY CREW AND I SAVED EARTH FROM THE **BORG**--

UM, SIR--?

Tom Tomorrow ©2015

THIS MODERN WORLD

by TOM TOMORROW

A THING JUST HAPPENED! WHAT IS YOUR OPINION?

WHAT?

THE THING THAT HAPPENED! FORM AN OPINION!

GIVE US A TAKE!

ER--WELL--

--THIS IS THE FIRST I'VE HEARD OF THE THING--BUT LET ME READ UP ON IT, AND THINK ABOUT IT FOR AWHILE, AND I'LL GET BACK TO YOU--

WHAT IS THIS, THE 14TH CENTURY?

THERE'S NO TIME FOR THAT!

YOU ARE EITHER FOR THE THING OR AGAINST THE THING!

PICK A SIDE! TAKE A STAND!

MAKE A SNAP JUDGMENT!

BUT--I MEAN, I DON'T KNOW ANYTHING ABOUT THE THING--

OH FOR CHRISSAKES.

NEVER MIND--

--A NEW THING JUST HAPPENED! WHAT DO YOU THINK ABOUT THAT?

UH--I AM OUTRAGED! AND/OR HIGHLY SUPPORTIVE.

NOW YOU'RE GETTING THE HANG OF IT.

TOM TOMORROW ©2015

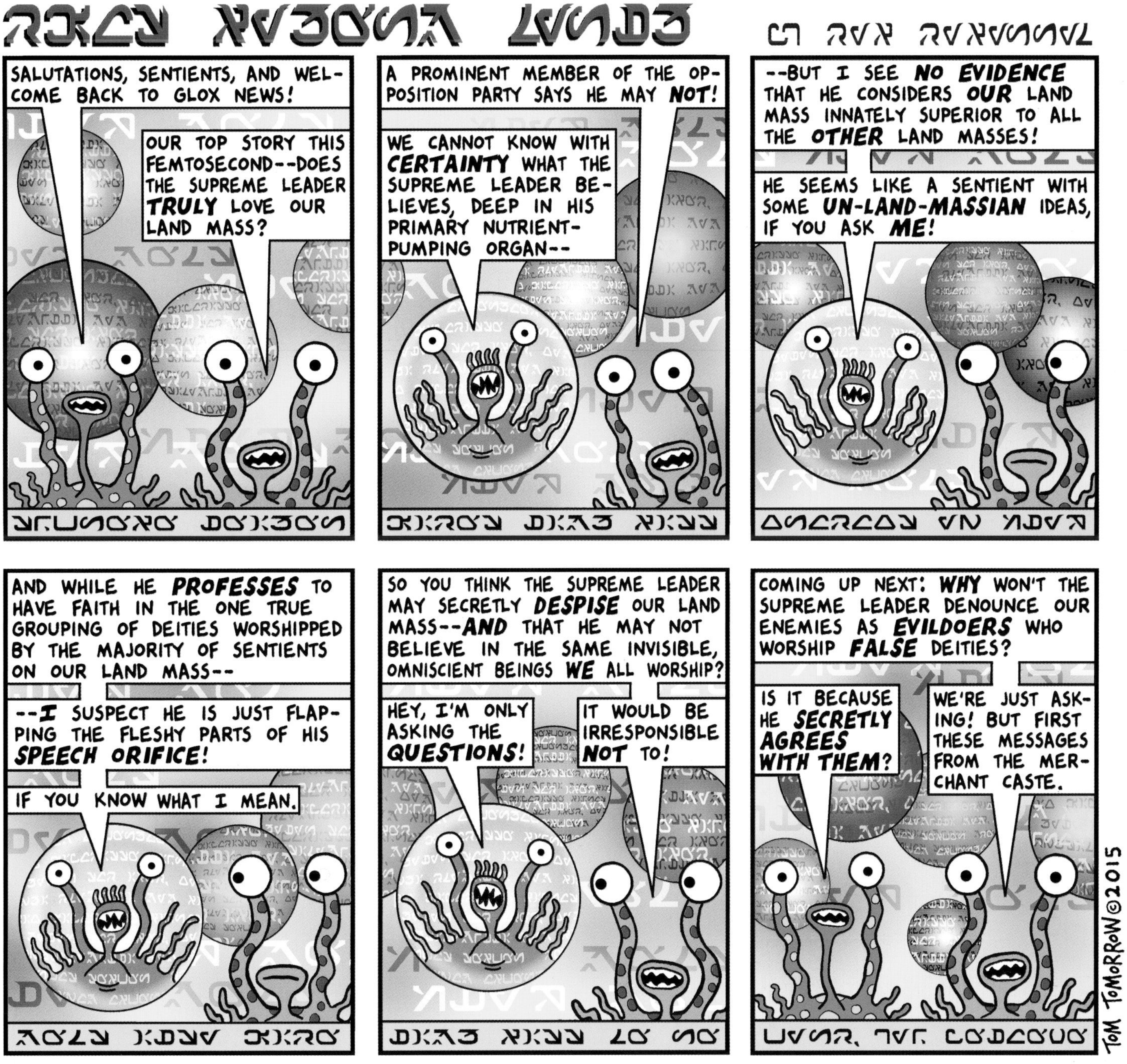
SALUTATIONS, SENTIENTS, AND WELCOME BACK TO GLOX NEWS!
OUR TOP STORY THIS FEMTOSECOND--DOES THE SUPREME LEADER TRULY LOVE OUR LAND MASS?
A PROMINENT MEMBER OF THE OPPOSITION PARTY SAYS HE MAY NOT!
WE CANNOT KNOW WITH CERTAINTY WHAT THE SUPREME LEADER BELIEVES, DEEP IN HIS PRIMARY NUTRIENT-PUMPING ORGAN--
--BUT I SEE NO EVIDENCE THAT HE CONSIDERS OUR LAND MASS INNATELY SUPERIOR TO ALL THE OTHER LAND MASSES!
HE SEEMS LIKE A SENTIENT WITH SOME UN-LAND-MASSIAN IDEAS, IF YOU ASK ME!
AND WHILE HE PROFESSES TO HAVE FAITH IN THE ONE TRUE GROUPING OF DEITIES WORSHIPPED BY THE MAJORITY OF SENTIENTS ON OUR LAND MASS--
--I SUSPECT HE IS JUST FLAPPING THE FLESHY PARTS OF HIS SPEECH ORIFICE!
IF YOU KNOW WHAT I MEAN.
SO YOU THINK THE SUPREME LEADER MAY SECRETLY DESPISE OUR LAND MASS--AND THAT HE MAY NOT BELIEVE IN THE SAME INVISIBLE, OMNISCIENT BEINGS WE ALL WORSHIP?
HEY, I'M ONLY ASKING THE QUESTIONS!
IT WOULD BE IRRESPONSIBLE NOT TO!
COMING UP NEXT: WHY WON'T THE SUPREME LEADER DENOUNCE OUR ENEMIES AS EVILDOERS WHO WORSHIP FALSE DEITIES?
IS IT BECAUSE HE SECRETLY AGREES WITH THEM?
WE'RE JUST ASKING! BUT FIRST THESE MESSAGES FROM THE MERCHANT CASTE.
TOM TOMORROW©2015

THIS MODERN WORLD
by TOM TOMORROW

THIS MODERN WORLD

by TOM TOMORROW

jk

REPUBLICAN AIDES SAY THE LETTER TO IRAN'S LEADERS WAS MEANT TO BE "LIGHTHEARTED" AND "CHEEKY"!

CHILL **OUT**, EVERYBODY! UNDER-MINING NUCLEAR NEGOTIATIONS WAS JUST A **JOKE!**

LIBERALS ARE **SO** HUMORLESS!

IT MAKES YOU WONDER WHAT **ELSE** OUR CONSERVATIVE FRIENDS HAVE BEEN JOSHING US ABOUT!

HA HA! DID YOU REALLY THINK WE WERE **SERIOUS** ABOUT DENYING CLIMATE CHANGE?

THAT STUNT WITH THE **SNOWBALL** DIDN'T TIP YOU OFF? WE'VE JUST BEEN **MESSING** WITH YOU!

MAYBE THE WHOLE BATTLE AGAINST **OBAMACARE** HAS BEEN ONE BIG ANDY KAUFMAN-ESQUE PERFORMANCE PIECE!

OBVIOUSLY THE MORE PEOPLE WE CAN GET INSURED, THE BETTER OFF WE ARE AS A SOCIETY!

WE REALLY HAD YOU **GOING** THOUGH, DIDN'T WE?

THE WAR ON WOMEN AND MINORITIES-- A BIG CRAZY **PRANK!**

GOOD LORD, WHAT KIND OF MONSTERS WOULD WE BE IF WE **ACTUALLY** THOUGHT WE SHOULD HAVE LEGAL AUTHORITY OVER A WOMAN'S RE-PRODUCTIVE HEALTH?

AND THAT WHOLE THING WHERE WE DENY THAT RACISM STILL EXISTS? SORRY! WE THOUGHT IT WAS **SELF-EVIDENTLY** SATIRE!

FOR THAT MATTER, INVADING IRAQ IN RESPONSE TO 9/11...?

I WAS **RIFFING!** I DIDN'T EXPECT EVERYONE TO TAKE ME **SERIOUSLY!**

GET A SENSE OF **HUMOR**, LIBTARDS!

LOL!

TOM TOMORROW ©2015

THIS MODERN WORLD

by TOM TOMORROW

HIGH-LIGHTS OF THE NEXT TWO YEARS

2015 — 2017

BROUGHT TO YOU IN ADVANCE THROUGH THE MIRACLE OF TOMORROW-VISION!

LUNATICS WITH NO HOPE OF EVER BECOMING PRESIDENT TREATED AS VIABLE CANDIDATES

AS PRESIDENT, I WILL NOT **REST**--

--UNTIL I FIND OBAMA'S **REAL** BIRTH CERTIFICATE!

TELL ME **MORE**!

ENDLESS DISCUSSION OF HILLARY CLINTON'S EMAIL ACCOUNT AND/OR OTHER MICROSCANDALS

A NIGERIAN PRINCE OFFERED HER A **FORTUNE**--BUT THERE'S **NO RECORD** OF HER **REPLY**!

WE MUST GET TO THE BOTTOM OF **NIGERIAN-PRINCEGATE**!

OR SHOULD WE SAY--NIGERIAN-PRINCE**GHAZI**?

MORE MISOGYNY THAN THE HUMAN MIND CAN COMPREHEND

A **FEMALE** DOESN'T HAVE WHAT IT **TAKES** TO BE PRESIDENT!

BY WHICH WE MEAN, A **PENIS**!

THE NOMINEES AND THE LONG SLOG TO THE FINISH LINE*

WILL IT BE **JEB** OR **HILLARY**?

HILLARY OR **JEB**?

JEB OR **HILLARY**?

HILLARY OR **JEB**?

ETC.

ETC.

ETC.

Action McNews Network

*DUE TO THE RELATIVE NATURE OF TIME, THIS PART LASTS ABOUT 53,000 YEARS

A HEALTHY PERSPECTIVE MAINTAINED BY ALL

YOU WROTE A CARTOON ABOUT **HILLARY**? DO YOU **WANT** THE REPUBLICANS TO WIN AND IMPOSE A THEOCRATIC DICTATORSHIP?

THAT'S CLEARLY THE ONLY LOGICAL CONCLUSION.

ALSO: CARTOONISTS CONTEMPLATE SHORT-TERM CRYOGENIC SUSPENSION

TOM TOMORROW ©2015

THIS MODERN WORLD

by TOM TOMORROW

TED CRUZ'S PATH TO THE WHITE HOUSE

STEP ONE: TED CRUZ ANNOUNCES HIS CANDIDACY.

I'M RUNNING FOR PRESIDENT-- BECAUSE OF *RONALD REAGAN!*

ALSO *GOD!*

AND *AMERICA!*

AND STUFF!

STEP TWO: ALL OTHER REPUBLICAN CONTENDERS ARE KILLED IN A FREAK MISHAP.

--AND THE ASTEROID CRASHED INTO THE DEBATE HALL, WIPING OUT THE ENTIRE G.O.P FIELD--

--EXCEPT FOR TED CRUZ, WHO WAS *MIRACULOUSLY SPARED!*

STEP THREE: CONGRESSIONAL REPUBLICANS FINALLY UNCOVER A SCANDAL THAT FORCES HILLARY CLINTON TO DROP OUT OF THE RACE.

WE HAVE INCONTROVERTIBLE *PROOF* THAT YOU DID THE SCANDALOUS THING, HILLARY CLINTON!

AND I'D HAVE GOTTEN *AWAY* WITH IT, TREY GOWDY--IF NOT FOR YOU MEDDLING *REPUBLICANS!*

STEP FOUR: DEMOCRATS FORGET TO NOMINATE A DIFFERENT CANDIDATE.

YOU'D *THINK* SOMEONE WOULD HAVE REMEMBERED--BUT IT JUST SLIPPED OUR MINDS!

BOY WERE *OUR* FACES RED WHEN ELECTION DAY ROLLED AROUND!

STEP FIVE: *VOILA!* TED CRUZ IS PRESIDENT.

IT IS A TOTALLY PLAUSIBLE THING THAT COULD HAPPEN.

SO YOU SHOULD PAY LOTS OF ATTENTION TO ME FOR THE NEXT EIGHTEEN MONTHS.

BECAUSE OF HOW I MIGHT WIN.

AND STUFF.

TOM TOMORROW ©2015

THIS MODERN WORLD

by TOM TOMORROW

Panel 1: HOWDY, EVERYONE--IT'S ME, *GOD!*

I KNOW I'M NOT WHAT SOME OF Y'ALL WERE *EXPECTIN'*--

I'M LOOKIN' AT *YOU,* UNITARIANS--

Panel 2: --BUT THE FACT IS, THE FUNDA-MENTALISTS GOT THINGS *EXACTLY RIGHT!* I'M *REAL*--AND I'M A *REPUBLICAN!*

SORRY LIBTARDS! SUCKS TO BE *YOU!*

Panel 3: AND I'LL TELL YOU SOMETHIN'--THOSE OL' BOYS IN ARKANSAS AND INDIANA WITH THEIR "RELIGIOUS FREEDOM" LAWS *TOTALLY* UNDER-STOOD WHAT MATTERS TO *ME!*

Panel 4: I MAY NOT PAY MUCH ATTENTION TO WARS AND PLANE CRASHES AND EBOLA OUTBREAKS AND WHATNOT--

--BUT I AM *VERY* CONCERNED ABOUT WHO DOES WHAT WITH THEIR *GENITALS!*

Panel 5: SPEAKIN' AS YOUR ALL-POWERFUL CREATOR, *NOTHIN'* GETS ME RILED UP LIKE THE THOUGHT OF SOME PASTRY CHEF BEIN' FORCED TO BAKE A CAKE FOR PEOPLE WHO DO NOT USE THEIR TALLYWACKERS AND THEIR HOO-HAWS IN A MANNER THAT I WOULD *PREFER!*

Panel 6: YESSIR, ONE OF THESE DAYS I'M GONNA DO SOME SERIOUS SMITING.

BUT RIGHT NOW IT'S TIME FOR *DUCK DYNASTY!*

I NEVER MISS AN EPISODE.

TOM TOMORROW ©2015

66

THIS MODERN WORLD

by TOM TOMORROW

OFFICER FRIENDLY! *ANOTHER* UNARMED BLACK MAN HAS BEEN KILLED BY A POLICE OFFICER--

--AND THE WHOLE THING WAS CAUGHT ON *VIDEO!*

THE OFFICER SHOOTS THE MAN IN THE BACK--AND THEN APPEARS TO PLANT *EVIDENCE!*

IF NOT FOR THE VIDEO, HE PROBABLY WOULD HAVE GOTTEN *AWAY* WITH IT!

IT MAKES YOU WONDER HOW OFTEN THINGS LIKE THIS *HAPPEN!*

NO IT DOESN'T.

BEG YOUR PARDON?

THIS WAS AN ISOLATED INCIDENT FROM WHICH *NO* LARGER CONCLUSIONS SHOULD BE DRAWN.

THAT COP WAS A *BAD APPLE* WHO'S ALREADY BEEN ARRESTED, AND I SEE *NO NEED* TO GIVE THE MATTER ANOTHER MOMENT'S THOUGHT.

SO YOU'RE SAYING THIS IS PROOF THAT THE SYSTEM *WORKS?*

SURE, AS LONG AS THERE'S A BYSTANDER WITH A PHONE CAMERA NEARBY.

WHICH THERE'S NOT, AT THE MOMENT.

UH--OKAY, THEN!

WE'LL BE GOING NOW.

TOM TOMORROW ©2015

THIS MODERN WORLD

by TOM TOMORROW

THE CAMPAIGN THAT ATE AMERICA'S BRAIN

DEEP IN ITS HIDDEN LAIR, THE ANCIENT CREATURE HUNGERED.

FEED ME PHOTO OPS...BANAL INSIGHTS...SHAMELESS PANDERING...RELIGIOUS PIETIES...OBSESSIVE COVERAGE OF INSIGNIFICANT DETAILS...

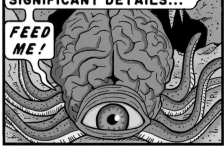

FEED ME!

AND SO, AN IRRESISTIBLE PSYCHIC COMMAND SWEPT ACROSS THE NATION.

LET THE PRESIDENTIAL CAMPAIGN...*COMMENCE!*

THEN...

HEY, ISN'T IT TIME FOR THE PRESIDENTIAL CAMPAIGN TO COMMENCE?

THE ELECTION *IS* A MERE NINETEEN MONTHS AWAY!

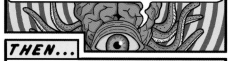

DRIVEN BY COMPULSIONS BEYOND HUMAN COMPREHENSION, CANDIDATES EAGERLY SUBMITTED TO A SUCCESSION OF RITUAL HUMILIATIONS.

I JUST *LOVE* GIANT COWS MADE OF BUTTER!

OUT OF MY WAY! *I* MUST POSE WITH THE BUTTER COW!

NO-- *ME!*

STATE FAIR

PUNDITS BABBLED CEASELESSLY, AND WITH GREAT AUTHORITY.

I FOUND HILLARY'S PROFESSED LOVE FOR THE BUTTER COW *ENTIRELY* UNCONVINCING.

I'LL BET SCOTT WALKER CARVES HIS *OWN* BUTTER COWS IN HIS SPARE TIME!

ORDINARY AMERICANS RELATE TO THINGS LIKE THAT!

AND NINETEEN MONTHS LATER AMERICANS AWAKENED, AS IF FROM A DREAM.

THE POLLS HAVE CLOSED-- AND THE NEXT PRESIDENT OF THE UNITED STATES *IS*--

WHAT-- WHAT JUST HAPPENED?

THE LAST THING *I* REMEMBER, IT WAS APRIL 2015!

UNFORTUNATELY, THE CREATURE'S APPETITES WERE INSATIABLE.

THE *NEXT* CAMPAIGN MUST BEGIN EVEN SOONER...

YES...MUCH, MUCH *SOONER!*

DEFINITELY NOT...*THE END!*

TOM TOMORROW ©2015

THIS MODERN WORLD

by TOM TOMORROW

DRONEY--I HEARD ON THE NEWS THAT TWO WESTERN **HOSTAGES** DIED IN A U.S. DRONE STRIKE LAST JANUARY!

THE NEW YORK TIMES SAYS THAT DRONE OPERATORS "OFTEN DO NOT KNOW WHO THEY ARE KILLING!"

THERE'S NOT MUCH RELIABLE DATA ON CIVILIAN CASUALTIES OF DRONES--

--BUT IN PAKISTAN ALONE, ESTIMATES RANGE FROM A FEW HUNDRED TO ALMOST A **THOUSAND!**

WHICH IS WEIRD, BECAUSE **YOU** KEEP TELLING US THAT DRONES ARE **SURGICALLY PRECISE!**

GUESS IT DEPENDS ON YOUR **SURGEON!** HEH, HEH!

NO? OH WELL.

LISTEN--MISTAKES WERE **MADE**, BY SOMEONE, SOMEWHERE! AND I'M SURE THOSE MISTAKES WILL BE ADDRESSED WITH **FULL TRANSPARENCY**, AT SOME UNSPECIFIED POINT IN THE INDETERMINATE FUTURE!

UNLESS THEY'RE NOT. WHO CAN **SAY?**

BUT HEY--ACCIDENTS **HAPPEN**, AMIRITE?

WHAT CAN YOU **DO?**

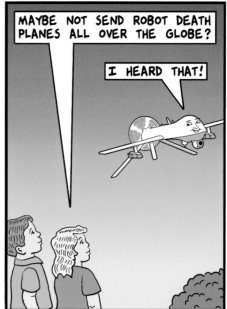

MAYBE NOT SEND ROBOT DEATH PLANES ALL OVER THE GLOBE?

I HEARD THAT!

TOM TOMORROW ©2015

THIS MODERN WORLD

by TOM TOMORROW

HELPFUL RESPONSES TO BALTIMORE*

*HELPFULNESS NOT GUARANTEED

1. PROTESTERS SHOULD BE MORE LIKE M.L.K.

BY WHICH WE MEAN, SAFELY CONTAINED IN THE PAST AND RELEGATED TO A FEW PLEASANT QUOTES TAKEN GLIBLY OUT OF CONTEXT!

THAT'S HOW YOU PROTEST INJUSTICE!

2. THE MAN WHO WAS BRUTALLY BEATEN TO DEATH BY POLICE HAD A CRIMINAL RECORD.

WE'RE NOT SAYING HE *DESERVED* WHAT HAPPENED--

WE'RE JUST STRONGLY *IMPLYING* IT!

3. THIS WAS YET ANOTHER ISOLATED INCIDENT FROM WHICH NO LARGER CONCLUSIONS SHOULD BE DRAWN.

ONE GUY GETS HIS LARYNX CRUSHED AND HIS SPINE SEVERED--

--AND *SOME* PEOPLE WON'T LET YOU HEAR THE *END* OF IT!

4. WE HAVE A BLACK PRESIDENT AND THEREFORE THIS IS ALL SOMEHOW HIS FAULT.

BLACK BLACK BLACKITY *BLACK!*

VERY, VERY BLACK.

ALSO, DID I MENTION *BLACK?*

5. RESPECT FOR AUTHORITY IS PARAMOUNT, EXCEPT WHEN IT'S NOT.

THESE LAWLESS PROTESTS ARE AN AFFRONT TO *DECENCY*--AND SHOULD NOT BE *TOLERATED!*

UNLESS THEY'RE PROTESTING GRAZING FEES, OF COURSE.

6. MAYBE FREDDIE GRAY'S INJURIES WERE SELF-INFLICTED.

IT *COULD* HAVE ALL BEEN A CUNNING SCHEME TO *DISCREDIT* THE *POLICE!*

WHAT A DIABOLICAL *MASTERMIND!*

7. THE REAL PROBLEM IS A LACK OF FAMILY VALUES.

FORGET ABOUT SYSTEMIC BRUTALITY AND ECONOMIC INEQUALITY!

LIFE IS SIMPLE WHEN YOU IGNORE THE COMPLICATED PARTS!

8. POOR PEOPLE IN BALTIMORE SHOULD JUST GET JOBS.

--AND IN AN ENTIRELY UNRELATED STORY, A NEW TRADE AGREEMENT IS LIKELY TO MAKE IT *EVEN EASIER* TO SHIP JOBS OVERSEAS!

FIRST THESE MESSAGES!

TOM TOMORROW ©2015

70

THIS MODERN WORLD

by TOM TOMORROW

SUPERHERO TEAM-UP COMICS

MIDDLE MAN

AND

INVISIBLE-HAND-OF-THE FREE-MARKET MAN

IF YOU'RE IN-VISIBLE--WHY CAN I **SEE** YOU?

NEVER MIND **THAT**-- WE'VE GOT A **TRADE DEAL** TO DEFEND!

TRANS-PACIFIC PARTNERSHIP

THIS ISH: THE **POPULIST MENACE!**

ONE RECENT AFTERNOON...

--AND IF YOU WANT TO HELP THE MIDDLE CLASS, YOU **MUST** MAKE IT EASIER TO SHIP THEIR JOBS **OVERSEAS!**

I SEE!

BUT SUDDENLY...

HOLD IT RIGHT THERE, MIDDLE-MAN! ARE YOU NEGOTIATING AN IMPORTANT TRADE AGREEMENT--IN **SECRET?**

POPULIST AVENGER! LOOK-- I **GOT** THIS! PEOPLE JUST HAVE TO **TRUST** ME!

YEAH! IF PEOPLE HAD LET HIM STRIKE A **GRAND BARGAIN,** WE COULD BE CUTTING **ENTITLEMENTS** BY NOW!

PERHAPS THIS IS NOT THE MOMENT FOR THAT DISCUSSION.

ANYWAY, THERE ARE NO **SECRETS** HERE! AT LEAST, THERE WON'T BE, ONCE WE'RE THROUGH WITH OUR SECRET NEGOTIATIONS!

AND IF CONGRESS WILL JUST **FAST TRACK** THE DEAL--YOU AND YOUR COLLEAGUES WILL STILL HAVE THE POWER TO REJECT IT **OUTRIGHT**--

:COUGH: WACKO LEFT-WING ISOLA-TIONISTS :COUGH:

--**OR** TO APPROVE IT AS NEGOTIATED, WITH **NO** CHANGES OR AMENDMENTS!

IT'S DEMOCRACY IN **ACTION**-- JUST SLIGHTLY **STREAMLINED!**

ANY-HOO--THANKS FOR STOPPING BY! WE'LL **DEFINITELY** KEEP YOU POSTED!

YOU HAVEN'T HEARD THE **LAST** OF THIS!

A FEW MOMENTS **LATER**...

I THOUGHT SHE'D NEVER **LEAVE!** LET'S GET BACK TO **WORK!**

IT'S TIME TO REACH ACROSS THE AISLE-- AND **GET THINGS DONE!**

TO BE **CONTINUED!**

TOM TOMORROW ©2015

THIS MODERN WORLD

by TOM TOMORROW

MISTER PENGUIN--DON'T YOU AGREE THAT THE MURDERED CARTOONISTS WERE UNNECESSARILY *VULGAR* AND *OFFENSIVE*?

YES--WASN'T THEIR WORK IN *EXTREMELY* POOR TASTE?

Action McNews Network

MAYBE SO! BUT THE PEOPLE WHO THINK IT'S A COOL IDEA TO KILL CARTOONISTS AREN'T SENSITIVE *ART CRITICS*, THOUGHTFULLY DETERMINING WHETHER CARTOONS PUNCH *UP* OR *DOWN*--

SPARKY T. PENGUIN
Obscure Cartoon Character

--THEY'RE EXTREMISTS LOOKING FOR INVENTIVE NEW WAYS TO CONDUCT ASYMMETRICAL WARFARE-- AND UNFORTUNATELY, CARTOONISTS ARE *VERY* SOFT TARGETS.

NONETHELESS--WEREN'T THE CARTOONS IN QUESTION *DREADFULLY* UNPLEASANT?

WELL-- AS I SAY--

Action McNews

BAM BAM BAM

--URK--

THUD!

Action McNews Network

I NEVER REALLY LIKED HIS CARTOONS ANYWAY.

TOO MANY WORDS.

Action McNews Network

Tom Tomorrow ©2015

THIS MODERN WORLD

by TOM TOMORROW

Panel 1:

WHAT HAPPENED--WHERE *AM* I--?

I'M AFRAID YOUR MORTAL EXISTENCE CAME TO AN ABRUPT CONCLUSION--AND YOU ENDED UP HERE--IN *HELL*!

Panel 2:

I HAVE TO ADMIT, I DIDN'T SEE THAT ONE COMING. BUT YOU KNOW, IT'S ALMOST A RELIEF.

HOW'S THAT, EXACTLY?

WELL--I WAS ABOUT TO PLUNGE INTO THE ABYSS OF ANOTHER INTERMINABLE CAMPAIGN CYCLE--

Panel 3:

--WATCHING DOZENS OF UNELECTABLE LUNATICS VIE FOR THE REPUBLICAN NOMINATION--AND TRYING TO FIND SOMETHING MORE INTERESTING TO SAY THAN, "HEY! LOOK AT ALL THE LUNATICS!"--

Panel 4:

--WHILE DEALING WITH HYPER-CAUTIOUS DEMOCRATS WHO SEEM TO THINK THAT CARTOONS ABOUT *THEIR* LIKELY CANDIDATE WILL LEAD DIRECTLY TO THE IMPOSITION OF A RIGHT-WING THEOCRACY!

Panel 5:

IT'S LIKE BEING TRAPPED IN A REAL-LIFE COMMENTS THREAD--WITH NO POSSIBILITY OF *ESCAPE*!

BUT HEY, I GUESS THAT'S NOT MY PROBLEM ANY MORE. SO WHAT UNENDING TORMENT DO *YOU* HAVE PLANNED FOR ME?

Panel 6:

--AND THEN I WOKE UP BACK IN MY OWN BED.

MAYBE YOU SHOULD GO EASY ON THE LATE NIGHT SNACKS.

TOM TOMORROW ©2015

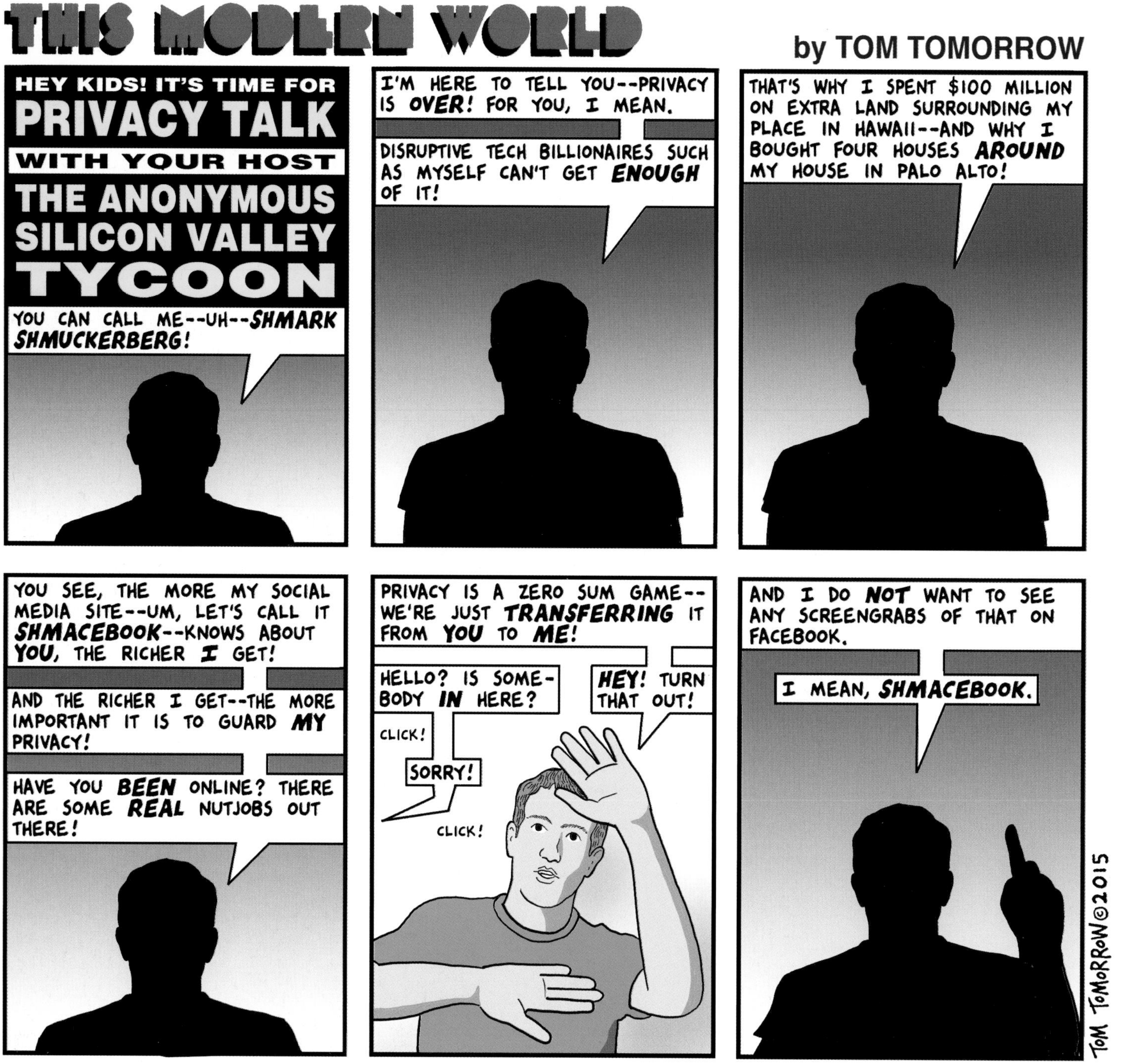
THIS MODERN WORLD
by TOM TOMORROW
HEY KIDS! IT'S TIME FOR
PRIVACY TALK
WITH YOUR HOST
THE ANONYMOUS SILICON VALLEY TYCOON
YOU CAN CALL ME--UH--SHMARK SHMUCKERBERG!
I'M HERE TO TELL YOU--PRIVACY IS OVER! FOR YOU, I MEAN.
DISRUPTIVE TECH BILLIONAIRES SUCH AS MYSELF CAN'T GET ENOUGH OF IT!
THAT'S WHY I SPENT $100 MILLION ON EXTRA LAND SURROUNDING MY PLACE IN HAWAII--AND WHY I BOUGHT FOUR HOUSES AROUND MY HOUSE IN PALO ALTO!
YOU SEE, THE MORE MY SOCIAL MEDIA SITE--UM, LET'S CALL IT SHMACEBOOK--KNOWS ABOUT YOU, THE RICHER I GET!
AND THE RICHER I GET--THE MORE IMPORTANT IT IS TO GUARD MY PRIVACY!
HAVE YOU BEEN ONLINE? THERE ARE SOME REAL NUTJOBS OUT THERE!
PRIVACY IS A ZERO SUM GAME--WE'RE JUST TRANSFERRING IT FROM YOU TO ME!
HELLO? IS SOME-BODY IN HERE?
HEY! TURN THAT OUT!
CLICK!
SORRY!
CLICK!
AND I DO NOT WANT TO SEE ANY SCREENGRABS OF THAT ON FACEBOOK.
I MEAN, SHMACEBOOK.
TOM TOMORROW©2015

THIS MODERN WORLD

by TOM TOMORROW

Russian "Troll Farms" Flooding the Internet with Pro-Kremlin Propaganda

HELLO! I AM BEAUTIFUL AMERICAN SWIMSUIT MODEL WHO LOVES APPLE PIE, AMERICAN FLAG, POPULAR TELEVISION PROGRAMS--

--AND *VLADIMIR PUTIN!*

HEH HEH

TAP TAP TAP

AMERICANS REALIZED THEY'D BEEN CAUGHT NAPPING.

THE RUSSIANS ARE LEAVING US IN THE *DUST!* IT'S JUST LIKE *SPUT-NIK*--EXCEPT WITH *TROLLS!*

WE MUST SPARE *NO* EXPENSE TO CLOSE THE *TROLL GAP!*

THE PRESIDENT ANNOUNCED A NEW NATIONAL INITIATIVE.

--AND SO, WE CHOOSE TO TROLL *HARDER* THAN THE RUSSIANS EVER COULD--

--NOT BECAUSE IT IS EASY--BUT BECAUSE THERE ARE *LULZ!*

A RAGTAG CREW WAS ASSEMBLED.

YOU MEN ARE THE BEST OF THE WORST AT MANSPLAINING, DOXXING, AND ANONYMOUS HARASSMENT! NOW WE WANT YOU TO USE THOSE SKILLS FOR YOUR *COUNTRY!*

CONSIDER THE RUSSKIES *PWNED*, SIR!

BATTLES WERE FOUGHT...CASUALTIES INCURRED...

MY CARPAL TUNNEL IS *REALLY* ACTING UP! YOU GUYS ARE GONNA HAVE TO GO ON WITHOUT ME!

WE WON'T DO IT, SARGE! WE *NEVER* LEAVE A MAN BEHIND!

THAT'S A *DIRECT ORDER*, SON.

NOW HAS ANY-ONE SEEN THE *IBUPROFEN*?

TROLLING

BUT IN THE END, THE RUSSIANS NEVER HAD A CHANCE AGAINST OUR BOYS.

WHAT DOES IT MEAN, "ETHICS IN GAMING JOURNALISM?"

UH OH...

HUGE TIP O' THE PEN(GUIN) TO JEET HEER!

TOM TOMORROW ©2015

75

THIS MODERN WORLD

by TOM TOMORROW

Panel 1: OUR TOP STORY--A WHITE POLICE OFFICER HAS ONCE AGAIN DONE AN INDEFENSIBLE THING TO A BLACK CITIZEN!

HERE TO DEFEND THE INDEFENSIBLE THING IS OUR FREQUENT GUEST, THE *SHAMELESS APOLOGIST!*

Panel 2: BETTY, THE INDEFENSIBLE THING WAS *CLEARLY* DEFENSIBLE! THE ISSUE ISN'T POLICE MISCONDUCT-- THE ISSUE IS *RAP MUSIC* AND *BAGGY PANTS!*

IF YOU KNOW WHAT I MEAN.

Panel 3: THANKS FOR YOUR INSIGHT, SHAMELESS APOLOGIST! AND NOW WE GO LIVE TO THE SCENE, WHERE OUR CORRESPONDENT HAS BEEN *INVESTIGATING* THE BLACK CITIZEN TO WHOM THE INDEFENSIBLE THING HAPPENED!

Panel 4: BIFF, I'M HERE ON THE STREET NEAR THE SCENE OF THE INDEFENSIBLE ACT--AND FROM WHAT I'VE BEEN TOLD, THE BLACK CITIZEN IN QUESTION WAS *NO ANGEL!*

WELL *THAT* CERTAINLY PUTS THINGS IN PERSPECTIVE!

Panel 5: AND NOW A SPECIAL EDITORIAL COMMENT FROM A *CRANKY OLD MAN!*

THERE'S NO RESPECT FOR LAW AND ORDER THESE DAYS! *I* THINK WE SHOULD LOCK UP ALL THE CRIMINALS AND THROW AWAY THE *KEY!* IN FACT--

EXCUSE ME-- ONE MOMENT--

Panel 6: --WE'VE GOT BREAKING NEWS-- *ANOTHER* POLICE OFFICER HAS DONE *ANOTHER* INDEFENSIBLE THING TO *ANOTHER* BLACK CITIZEN!

BOY, WHAT WERE THE ODDS OF *THAT?*

WE'LL EXPLAIN WHY THE VICTIM WAS TO BLAME--AS SOON AS WE GET *MORE DETAILS!*

GO BACK TO BEGINNING AND START OVER...AND OVER AND OVER AND OVER...

TOM TOMORROW ©2015

THIS MODERN WORLD

by TOM TOMORROW

A CONFEDERACY OF DENIAL

GUNS AREN'T A PROBLEM IN THIS COUNTRY!

AND RACISM IS A THING OF THE PAST!

ALSO THERE'S NO GLOBAL WARMING.

DUH.

1) WE MUSTN'T POLITICIZE THE TRAGEDY.

IT'S MUCH TOO SOON TO START CASTING BLAME!

I'D SUGGEST WAITING A COUPLE OF DECADES-- TO MAKE SURE WE HAVE SUFFICIENT DISTANCE!

2) WE SHOULDN'T ALLOW OURSELVES TO BE SIDETRACKED.

JUST BECAUSE A WHITE SUPREMACIST OPENED FIRE IN A HISTORIC BLACK CHURCH WHILE DENOUNCING BLACK PEOPLE--

--I DON'T SEE WHY WE HAVE TO MAKE THE WHOLE THING ABOUT RACE!

3) OBVIOUSLY, THIS PROVES WE NEED MORE GUNS.

HOW CAN WE PROTECT OURSELVES FROM ALL THE NUTJOBS WALKING AROUND WITH GUNS OUT THERE--

--UNLESS EVERYONE IS HEAVILY ARMED AT ALL TIMES?

4) LIBERALS ARE SOMEHOW TO BLAME.

YOU KNOW, WITH THEIR--UM-- PERMISSIVENESS, AND EVERY- THING.

WE MIGHT NEED TO WORK ON THIS ONE.

5) AND OF COURSE--THIS WAS JUST ANOTHER ISOLATED INCIDENT, FROM WHICH NO GREATER CONCLUSIONS SHOULD BE DRAWN.

THAT'S RIGHT! AN UNFATHOMABLE ACT, ENTIRELY DEVOID OF CONTEXT-- AS USUAL!

I BLAME "EVIL."

YES--"EVIL" IS VERY BAD!

TOM TOMORROW ©2015

THIS MODERN WORLD

by TOM TOMORROW

CAMPAIGN 2016

THE LONG, LONG, *LONG* RACE FOR THE WHITE HOUSE

THIS WEEK: JEB BUSH!

OR AS WE LIKE TO CALL HIM, JOHN ELLIS BUSH-BUSH!

IT'S OFFICIAL--JOHN ELLIS BUSH-BUSH IS RUNNING FOR *PRESIDENT!*

AND CAN'T YOU JUST *FEEL* THE JEB-*MENTUM?*

NOT TO MENTION THE JEB-*CITEMENT?*

I'M SIMPLY TINGLING WITH... JEB-*TICIPATION!*

HE WANTS TO BE AN INSPIRATION FOR *ALL* AMERICANS!

THIS IS A FANTASTIC LAND OF OPPORTUNITY, WHERE *ANYONE* CAN BE BORN INTO A POLITICAL DYNASTY!

UNLESS YOU'RE NOT.

HE MAY BE THE ULTIMATE INSIDER-- BUT HE *IDENTIFIES* AS A PLUCKY *OUTSIDER!*

"THE PRESIDENCY SHOULD NOT BE PASSED ALONG FROM ONE *LIBERAL* TO THE NEXT!"

"WE DON'T NEED ANOTHER PRESIDENT WHO MERELY HOLDS THE TOP SPOT AMONG THE *PAMPERED ELITES* OF *WASHINGTON!"*

Jeb!

*WORDS THAT ACTUALLY CAME OUT OF JOHN ELLIS BUSH-BUSH'S MOUTH!

ARE REPUBLICANS *READY* TO GET BEHIND ANOTHER BUSH?

HIS BROTHER GAVE US TWO WARS, THE PATRIOT ACT, NSA SURVEILLANCE AND TORTURE AS AN OFFICIAL GOVERNMENT POLICY--

--BUT SINCE WE DON'T CONSIDER ANY OF THOSE THINGS *MISTAKES*, IT'S NOT REALLY A *PROBLEM!*

BUT WAIT--WHAT'S *THIS?* AN EVEN *MORE* INSPIRING CANDIDATE?

Sorry losers and haters, but my I.Q. is one of the highest -and you all know it! Please don't feel so stupid or insecure, it's not your fault

ACTUAL TWEET FROM 2013!

TRULY, THE REPUBLICAN FIELD IS AN *EMBARRASSMENT* OF RICHES!

NEXT: I'M A BOX OF *ROCKS*--AND I WANT TO BE *YOUR* PRESIDENT!

I THINK HE'S REALLY GOT WHAT IT *TAKES!*

TOM TOMORROW ©2015

78

THIS MODERN WORLD

by TOM TOMORROW

THEY AWOKE TO FIND...

A WORLD GONE MAD

A RISING GROUNDSWELL AGAINST THE *CONFEDERATE FLAG!*

BUT--IT'S NOT ABOUT *HATE*--IT'S ABOUT *HERITAGE!*

ADMITTEDLY, A HIGHLY SELECTIVE HERITAGE THAT DOES NOT ACKNOWLEDGE SLAVERY, LYNCHING, OR SEGREGATION.

LET US NOT FIXATE ON *DETAILS!*

GAY MARRIAGE UPHELD BY THE *SUPREME COURT!*

WHAT'S *NEXT*--MEN WITH *MULTIPLE WIVES?*

YOU MEAN LIKE IN THE BIBLE?

WHAT?

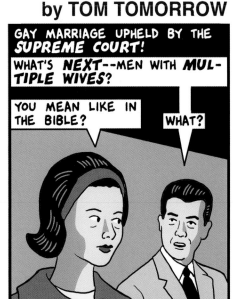

CONSERVATIVES WERE UNDER *ATTACK!*

PEOPLE WHO BELIEVE THEIR RELIGION REQUIRES THEM TO DENY OTHER PEOPLE BASIC CIVIL RIGHTS ARE THE *REAL* VICTIMS HERE!

NOT TO *MENTION* PEOPLE WHO WANT TO FLY A PERFECTLY INNOCENT FLAG INEXPLICABLY ASSOCIATED WITH RACISM!

AT LEAST *SOME* SANITY PREVAILED!

WE FIND IN *FAVOR* OF TORTUROUS EXECUTION BY EXPERIMENTAL DRUGS!

"WHILE MOST HUMANS *WISH* TO DIE A PAINLESS DEATH--MANY DO NOT HAVE THAT GOOD FORTUNE!"

JUSTICE ALITO ACTUALLY WROTE THIS!

AS ALITO ALSO NOTED: "BECAUSE IT IS SETTLED THAT CAPITAL PUNISHMENT IS CONSTITUTIONAL--"

"--IT NECESSARILY FOLLOWS THAT THERE MUST BE A CONSTITUTIONAL MEANS OF CARRYING IT OUT!"

SUCH AS DEATH BY *HEAD EXPLODINGLY FACILE LOGIC!*

THAT'S NOT JUDICIAL REASONING-- *YAARGH!*

--IT'S JUST A CRUEL TAUTOLOGY!-- *BLAAGH!*

HEY! CHECK OUT MY KICKSTARTER: WWW.MAKETHATTHING.COM/TMW25

TOM TOMORROW ©2015

79

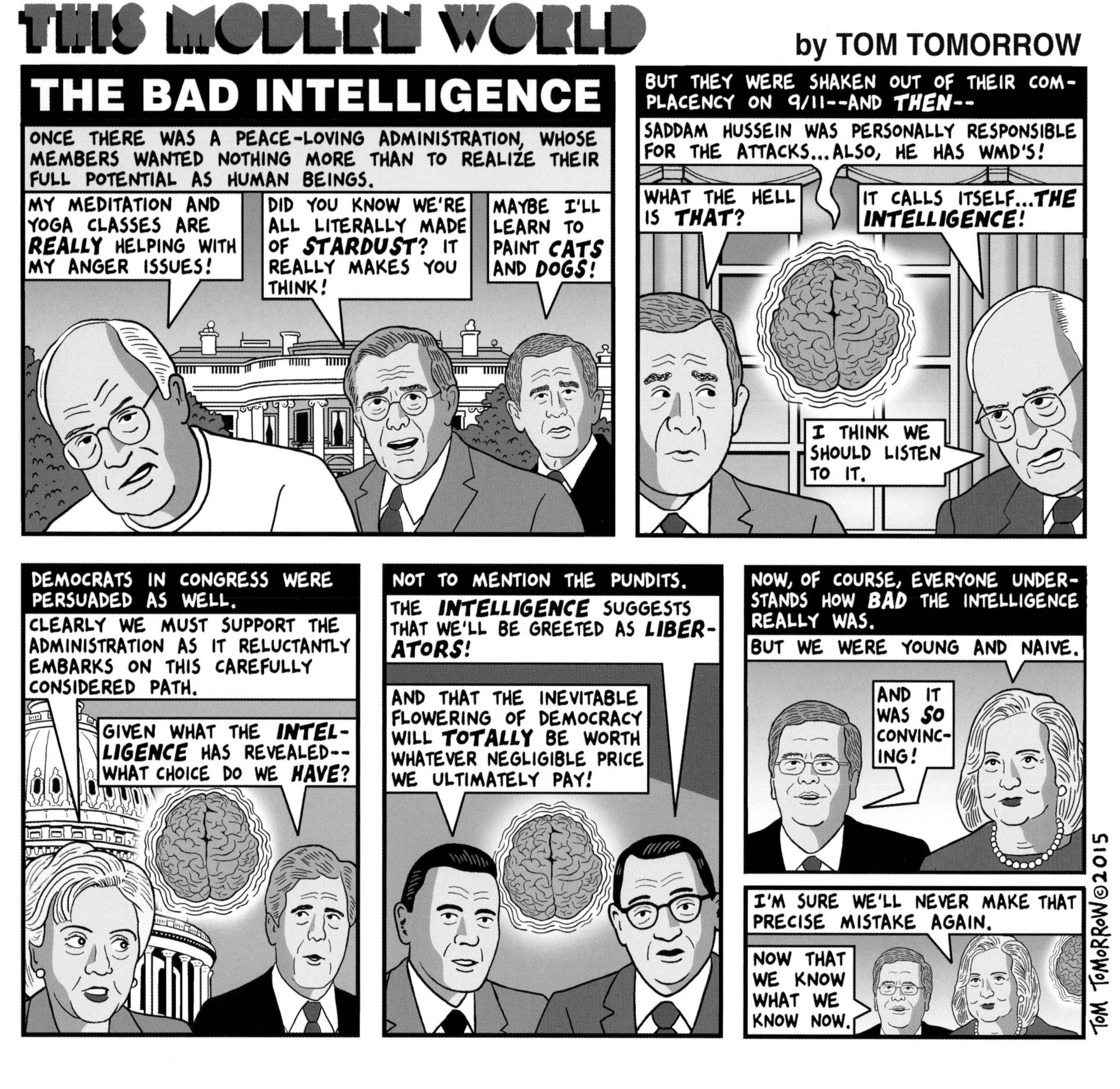
THIS MODERN WORLD
by TOM TOMORROW
THE BAD INTELLIGENCE
ONCE THERE WAS A PEACE-LOVING ADMINISTRATION, WHOSE MEMBERS WANTED NOTHING MORE THAN TO REALIZE THEIR FULL POTENTIAL AS HUMAN BEINGS.
MY MEDITATION AND YOGA CLASSES ARE REALLY HELPING WITH MY ANGER ISSUES!
DID YOU KNOW WE'RE ALL LITERALLY MADE OF STARDUST? IT REALLY MAKES YOU THINK!
MAYBE I'LL LEARN TO PAINT CATS AND DOGS!
BUT THEY WERE SHAKEN OUT OF THEIR COMPLACENCY ON 9/11--AND THEN--
SADDAM HUSSEIN WAS PERSONALLY RESPONSIBLE FOR THE ATTACKS...ALSO, HE HAS WMD'S!
WHAT THE HELL IS THAT?
IT CALLS ITSELF...THE INTELLIGENCE!
I THINK WE SHOULD LISTEN TO IT.
DEMOCRATS IN CONGRESS WERE PERSUADED AS WELL.
CLEARLY WE MUST SUPPORT THE ADMINISTRATION AS IT RELUCTANTLY EMBARKS ON THIS CAREFULLY CONSIDERED PATH.
GIVEN WHAT THE INTELLIGENCE HAS REVEALED--WHAT CHOICE DO WE HAVE?
NOT TO MENTION THE PUNDITS.
THE INTELLIGENCE SUGGESTS THAT WE'LL BE GREETED AS LIBERATORS!
AND THAT THE INEVITABLE FLOWERING OF DEMOCRACY WILL TOTALLY BE WORTH WHATEVER NEGLIGIBLE PRICE WE ULTIMATELY PAY!
NOW, OF COURSE, EVERYONE UNDERSTANDS HOW BAD THE INTELLIGENCE REALLY WAS.
BUT WE WERE YOUNG AND NAIVE.
AND IT WAS SO CONVINCING!
I'M SURE WE'LL NEVER MAKE THAT PRECISE MISTAKE AGAIN.
NOW THAT WE KNOW WHAT WE KNOW NOW.
TOM TOMORROW©2015

THIS MODERN WORLD

by TOM TOMORROW

THE ALIEN TRANSMISSION TOOK EVERYONE BY SURPRISE.

ATTENTION EARTHLINGS! WE HEREBY CLAIM YOUR WORLD FOR OURSELVES! OUR NANOBOTS HAVE ALREADY BEGUN TRANSFORMING YOUR ECOSYSTEM TO BETTER SUIT OUR NEEDS!

THE PROCESS WILL TAKE APPROXIMATELY FIVE OF YOUR EARTH YEARS--AT WHICH POINT YOUR PLANET WILL NO LONGER SUSTAIN HUMAN LIFE!

WE REGRET ANY INCONVENIENCE THIS MAY CAUSE.

THE APPROPRIATE RESPONSE SEEMED OBVIOUS.

WE MUST SET ASIDE OUR PETTY DIFFERENCES AND WORK TOGETHER TO **DEFEAT** THIS MENACE!

POLITICAL DISAGREEMENTS WON'T MATTER WITHOUT A PLANET TO **HAVE** THEM ON!

BUT REPUBLICANS IN CONGRESS WEREN'T BUYING ANY OF IT.

I DON'T CARE **WHAT** THE SCIENTISTS THINK! THE **BIBLE** DOESN'T SAY ANYTHING ABOUT THESE SO-CALLED **ALIENS!**

IT'S ADAM AND EVE, NOT ADAM AND WEIRD GREEN TENTACLE GUY!

DENYING THE THREAT BECAME A MATTER OF TRIBAL IDENTITY FOR MANY.

SURE, THERE'S A LITTLE MORE **CYANIDE** IN THE ATMOSPHERE-- AND THE OCEANS ARE STRANGELY **GELATINOUS**--

--BUT THAT DOESN'T PROVE THAT OUR WORLD IS BEING RECONFIGURED BY ALIEN **NANOBOTS!**

NO MATTER **WHAT** AL GORE THINKS!

HEH HEH.

OTHERS JUST TRIED NOT TO THINK ABOUT IT TOO MUCH.

WE'VE STILL GOT **PLENTY** OF TIME TO ADAPT! SOMEHOW.

IF THE TECH INDUSTRY CAN GIVE US APPS LIKE **UBER** AND **TINDER**-- I'M SURE THEY CAN SOLVE **THIS** PROBLEM TOO!

AND FIVE YEARS LATER--

I'VE NEVER SEEN A SPECIES GIVE UP SO EASILY.

WELL, THE PLACE IS DEFINITELY A FIXER-UPPER. HAVE YOU **SEEN** WHAT THEY DID TO THEIR OWN CLIMATE?

CHECK OUT MY KICKSTARTER FOR GIANT TWO VOLUME 25 **YEARS OF TOMORROW!** WWW.MAKETHATTHING.COM/TMW25

TOM TOMORROW©2015

THIS MODERN WORLD

by TOM TOMORROW

OBLIGATORY DONALD TRUMP CARTOON

WHADDYA MEAN, "OBLIGATORY"? YOU OUGHTA BE *GRATEFUL*!

THIS LOUSY CARTOON GETS CLASSIER JUST BY MENTIONING MY *NAME*!

PUNDITS AGREE--HE IS DEFINITELY *OUTRAGEOUS*!

DID YOU HEAR THE LATEST OUTRAGEOUS THING HE *SAID*?

IT WAS *VERY* OUTRAGEOUS! HE IS CERTAINLY A GIFT TO HUMORISTS, WITH ALL THE OUTRAGEOUSNESS!

AND YET HE LEADS THE REPUBLICAN PACK!

IN THE MIDDLE OF SUMMER, 16 MONTHS BEFORE THE ELECTION, THE WEIRDLY ENTERTAINING CELEBRITY WITH NO APPARENT FILTER IS GETTING THE MOST *ATTENTION*?

BE RIGHT BACK--GOTTA WRITE A THINKPIECE ABOUT WHAT IT ALL *MEANS*!

AT LEAST--UNTIL AN UNEXPECTED TURN OF *EVENTS*!

--SO YOU SEE, HIS HAIR WASN'T REALLY HAIR AT *ALL*--BUT RATHER, AN ALIEN PARASITE CONTROLLING HIS EVERY ACTION FOR DECADES!

I'M SO SORRY FOR ALL THOSE TERRIBLE THINGS MY HAIR MADE ME SAY!

YOU'RE ALL *FIRED*!

FREED FROM HIS HATEFUL *HAIR*, TRUMP IS A *CHANGED MAN*.

WE MUST NOT SCAPEGOAT THOSE WHO CROSS ARBITRARY BORDERS IN SEARCH OF A BETTER LIFE--LEST WE LOSE SIGHT OF OUR OWN *HUMANITY*!

WAIT, WHUT?

OBVIOUSLY HIS SUPPORTERS SOON EMBRACE A *NEW* CANDIDATE.

UGG MIGHTY *WARRIOR*! UGG SMASH *ENEMIES*!

FORGET *TRUMP*! ME VOTE *UGG*!

HEY! THERE'S NOT MUCH TIME LEFT ON MY KICKSTARTER FOR A HUGE, TWO-VOLUME HARDCOVER COLLECTION OF *EVERY TMW CARTOON!* WWW.MAKETHATTHING.COM/TMW25

TOM TOMORROW ©2015

THIS MODERN WORLD

by TOM TOMORROW

THINGS DONALD TRUMP COULD DO TO LOOK EVEN MORE PRESIDENTIAL

ANOTHER IN A SERIES OF UNAVOIDABLE CARTOONS ABOUT TERRIBLE PEOPLE WHO ARE NEVER ACTUALLY GOING TO BE PRESIDENT

1. NOTHING SAYS "LEADERSHIP" LIKE PETTY, VINDICTIVE BEHAVIOR--SO HE SHOULD *DEFINITELY* DOUBLE DOWN ON *THAT!*

IF SOMEONE MESSES WITH *ME*, I'LL SUE THEM FOR EVERYTHING THEY'VE *GOT*--AND/OR CALL THEM NAMES ON *TWITTER!*

THERE'S A MAN WHO CAN HANDLE VLADIMIR PUTIN!

2. HE SAID HE'D LOVE TO GIVE *SARAH PALIN* A CABINET SPOT-- BUT PERHAPS THERE ARE EVEN *LESS* POPULAR AMERICANS HE COULD CONSIDER!

THAT GUY WHO SHOT THE LION WOULD BE AN *EXCELLENT* SECRETARY OF THE INTERIOR!

THAT'S SOME OUT-OF-THE-BOX THINKING!

3. WHAT IF HE LOCKED ALL THE OTHER G.O.P. CANDIDATES IN A VACUUM CHAMBER--AND *LITERALLY* SUCKED ALL THE OXYGEN OUT OF THE ROOM!

IT'S WHAT THEY ALL *SAY* I'M DOING ANYWAY! HEH HEH!

LOOK AT THEM TURNING BLUE IN THERE--THE *LOSERS!*

4. JUST FOR THE HELL OF IT, HE COULD BITE THE HEAD OFF A LIVE CHICKEN DURING THE NEXT PRESIDENTIAL DEBATE.

I'M *DONALD TRUMP*, BITCHES! THE RULES DON'T *APPLY* TO *ME!*

WHAT A *MAVERICK!*

NOBODY TELLS *HIM* WHAT TO DO!

5. THEN AGAIN, MAYBE THERE IS NOTHING DONALD TRUMP COULD DO TO LOOK MORE PRESIDENTIAL THAN HE ALREADY DOES.

WE NEED A GIANT *WALL* AROUND THE COUNTRY! OR BETTER YET, AN IMPENETRABLE *DOME!*

THAT WILL KEEP THE MEXICAN RAPISTS OUT!

YARGLE BARGLE!

BLARGH!

TOM TOMORROW ©2015

83

THIS MODERN WORLD

by TOM TOMORROW

SO WHAT DOES THE SIMULACRON-2 **DO**, DR. VON PHILBERT?

WELL, BILLY--I'VE PRO-GRAMMED A **SIMULATED** VERSION OF OUR ENTIRE WORLD--POPULATED BY AUTONOMOUS UNITS WHO BELIEVE THEMSELVES TO BE ACTUAL PEOPLE LIVING IN A PHYSICAL UNIVERSE!

WHOA!

simulacron-2

WITHIN THIS VIRTUAL WORLD, I'VE BEEN RUNNING A TEST LASTING SEVERAL SUBJECTIVE DECADES--TO SEE HOW FAR A POLITICAL PARTY CAN DESCEND INTO **MADNESS** BEFORE IT FINALLY LOSES ALL LEGITIMACY!

simulacron-2

THE REPUBLICAN PARTY OF MY **SIMULATED** WORLD IS FULL OF GUN FETISHISTS, WHITE SUPREME-CISTS, MISOGYNISTS AND LUNATICS! WHY, MANY OF THEIR CORE VOTERS BELIEVE THE UNITED STATES GOV-ERNMENT IS SECRETLY PLOTTING TO INVADE **ITSELF**!

THAT'S CRAZY!

simulacron-2

OH, YOU SHOULD SEE THE **CAN-DIDATES** I'VE CREATED FOR THEM! THEY PREFER WAR TO DIPLOMACY, OPPOSE CLEAN AIR LAWS, WANT TO CRIMINALIZE ABORTION ENTIRELY, AND REFUSE TO ACKNOWLEDGE THE BASIC SCIENCE OF CLIMATE CHANGE!

AND THAT'S JUST FOR **STARTERS**!

simulacron-2

MY PIECE-DE-RESISTANCE IS A BLATANTLY RACIST AND SEXIST REALITY TV STAR WITH A REALLY BAD COMB-OVER--PROGRAMMED TO BEHAVE AS BOORISHLY AS **POSSIBLE**!

I PROBABLY GOT A LITTLE CARRIED AWAY WITH THAT ONE--BUT HE'S BEEN THE **FRONTRUNNER**!

WOW! I'M SURE GLAD HE'S JUST A **SIMULATION**!

simulacron-2

MEANWHILE, IN A REALITY ONE LEVEL **ABOVE**...

SO WHAT DOES THE SIMULACRON-3 **DO**?

WELL, BILLY--IT'S A SIMULATED VERSION OF OUR WORLD--BUT WITH A REPUBLICAN PARTY FULL OF **RATIONAL** PEOPLE!

HAH! IF ONLY!

simulacron-2

simulacron-3

TOM TOMORROW ©2015

84

THIS MODERN WORLD

by TOM TOMORROW

VOTER OUTREACH

HELLO, LADIES! I'M FROM THE REPUBLICAN PARTY--AND WE WANT YOUR **VOTES!**

LIKE I ALWAYS SAY, YOU CAN'T HAVE A PARTY WITHOUT SOME **LADIES!**

?

NOW, I KNOW--SOME OF YOU GALS GET UPSET BECAUSE WE'RE TRYING TO RESTRICT ACCESS TO ABORTION, AND EVEN MAKE IT AS DIFFICULT AS POSSIBLE TO GET BASIC **CONTRACEPTION**--

--AND THERE'S THAT WHOLE BUSINESS WITH THE FORCED **TRANSVAGINAL ULTRASOUNDS**--

--AND IT GOES WITHOUT **SAYING** THAT WE HAVE NO INTEREST IN LEGISLATING EQUAL PAY FOR EQUAL WORK--

--BUT WE **ARE** WILLING TO EXPRESS DISAPPROVAL OF THE **DREADFULLY** SEXIST THING SAID BY THE BOORISH BILLIONAIRE WE'RE DESPERATELY TRYING TO DRIVE OUT OF THE RACE.

I MEAN, UNLESS THERE'S A BACKLASH. I'M NOT MAKING ANY **PROMISES.**

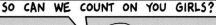

SO CAN WE COUNT ON YOU GIRLS?

I'LL TAKE YOUR HOSTILE SILENCE AS A "YES."

NOW WHICH ONE OF YOU LITTLE DARLINGS WANTS TO GO MAKE ME A **SANDWICH?**

HEH HEH.

TOM TOMORROW©2015

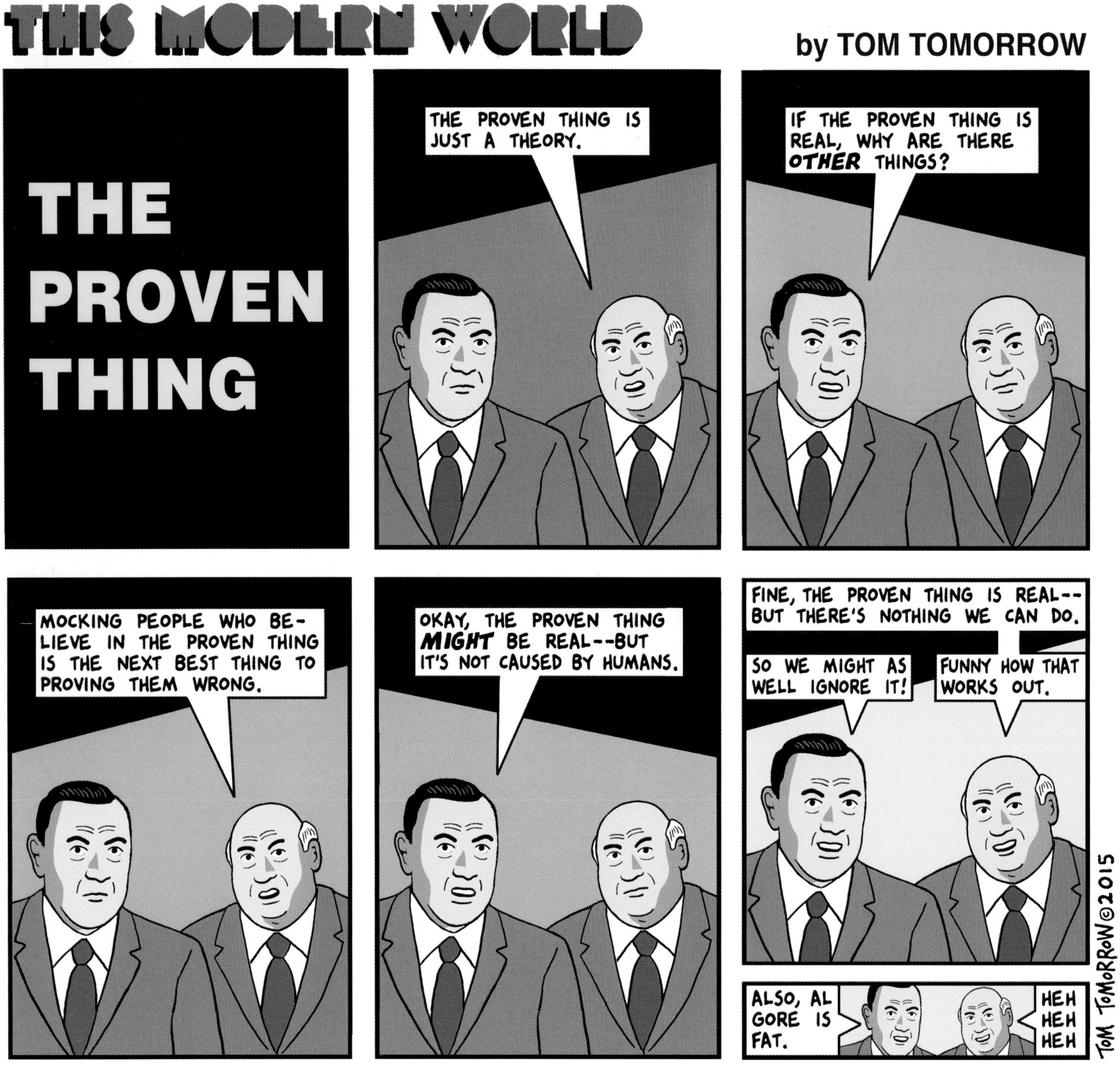
THIS MODERN WORLD
by TOM TOMORROW
THE PROVEN THING
THE PROVEN THING IS JUST A THEORY.
IF THE PROVEN THING IS REAL, WHY ARE THERE OTHER THINGS?
MOCKING PEOPLE WHO BE- LIEVE IN THE PROVEN THING IS THE NEXT BEST THING TO PROVING THEM WRONG.
OKAY, THE PROVEN THING MIGHT BE REAL--BUT IT'S NOT CAUSED BY HUMANS.
FINE, THE PROVEN THING IS REAL-- BUT THERE'S NOTHING WE CAN DO.
SO WE MIGHT AS WELL IGNORE IT!
FUNNY HOW THAT WORKS OUT.
ALSO, AL GORE IS FAT.
HEH HEH HEH
TOM TOMORROW©2015

THIS MODERN WORLD

by TOM TOMORROW

OKAY, SO HERE'S THE PART WHERE I EXPRESS MY OUTRAGE AT THE LATEST GUN MASSACRE.

AND HERE'S THE PART WHERE I DENOUNCE YOU FOR POLITICIZING THE TRAGEDY.

AND HERE'S THE PART WHERE I POINT OUT HOW OFTEN THESE THINGS HAPPEN IN AMERICA.

AND HERE'S THE PART WHERE I ARGUE THAT IT MEANS WE ACTUALLY NEED *MORE* GUNS.

ALL RIGHT, SEE YOU BACK HERE IN A COUPLE DAYS.

CAN YOU CLOCK US BOTH OUT?

SURE, NO PROBLEM.

TOM TOMORROW ©2015

SALUTATIONS, SENTIENTS! OUR TOP STORY THIS PICOSECOND--THE CENTRAL EXCHANGE THROUGH WHICH SHINY STONES ARE INVESTED IN CORPORATE ENTITIES SUFFERED GREAT TURMOIL THIS WEEK!
THE ASSIGNATION OF VALUE ROSE AND FELL LIKE A RIDE DESIGNED TO INDUCE SENSATIONS OF VERTIGO AND DISORIENTATION FOR PURPOSES OF AMUSEMENT!
TO HELP US COMPREHEND THE CAUSE OF THIS UPHEAVAL, WE'RE JOINED BY AN ESTEEMED FINANCIAL EXPERT!
WELL--IT COULD BE RELATED TO THE ARBITRARY VALUATION OF THE SHINY STONES ON OTHER LAND MASSES!
THEN AGAIN, IT COULD JUST BE THE INVISIBLE TENTACLE OF THE UNHINDERED EXCHANGE--ASSIGNING PROPER VALUE IN ITS OWN UNFATHOMABLE FASHION!
ONLY THE ONE TRUE GROUPING OF DEITIES KNOW FOR SURE!
INTERESTING! WHAT ADVICE DO YOU HAVE FOR ELDERLY SENTIENTS WHO HAVE INVESTED THEIR SHINY STONES IN THE EXCHANGE--IN HOPES OF SUSTAINING THEIR EXISTENCE AND AVOIDING BANISHMENT TO THE NORTHERNMOST PLAINS--
--WHERE THEY WILL INEVITABLY BE CONSUMED BY THE GREAT AND TERRIBLE BEASTS WHICH ROAM THERE?
I'D TELL THEM TO SUPPRESS THEIR ANXIETY!
YOU SEE, IF EVERYONE WITHDRAWS THEIR SHINY STONES FROM THE EXCHANGE AT ONCE, THE FUTURE VALUE OF THE CORPORATE ENTITIES IN WHICH WE INVEST COULD DECLINE PRECIPITOUSLY!
HOWEVER, IF EVERYONE CONTINUES TO BELIEVE IN THE VALUE OF THE EXCHANGE--THEN THE EXCHANGE WILL CONTINUE TO HAVE VALUE!
I SEE!
COMING UP NEXT: EXPERTS EXPLAIN WHY THIS IS A FUNDAMENTALLY RATIONAL ECONOMIC SYSTEM!
FIRST THESE DELIGHTFULLY INFORMATIVE MESSAGES FROM THE MERCHANT CLASS.
TOM TOMORROW©2015

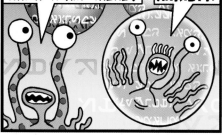

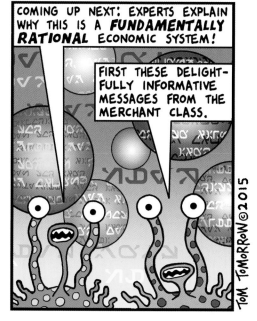

THIS MODERN WORLD

by TOM TOMORROW

Plutocrat Pete &
Tea Party Tim
in...

"The Breakup"

PREVIOUSLY...

WE HAVE TO **SAVE** OUR COUNTRY FROM THE ABORTIONISTS AND HOMO-SEXUALS AND FOREIGNERS--DON'T YOU **AGREE**, PLUTOCRAT PETE?

HMMM...

IF I CAN KEEP MORONS LIKE THIS RILED UP ABOUT POINTLESS SOCIAL ISSUES, THEY'LL TURN OUT IN **DROVES** TO VOTE THE WAY I WANT THEM TO! WHAT COULD GO **WRONG**?

HEH HEH HEH!

UM, IS SOME-THING FUNNY?

OH, UH--JUST A NERVOUS TIC! SAY, I'M **ALSO** VERY ANGRY ABOUT THE LIBERALS AND THE MINORITIES AND THE FEMINISTS AND SO ON!

BUT WHAT CAN WE **DO**?

NURTURE THAT RESENTMENT, YOUNG MAN! LET THE HATE FESTER INSIDE OF YOU UNTIL IT FEELS LIKE YOU'RE GOING TO **BURST** WITH RAGE!

AND THEN VOTE FOR THE CANDIDATES OF MY CHOOSING.

UM, OKAY. I GUESS.

BUT A FEW YEARS LATER...

DONALD TRUMP IS A **REAL** STRAIGHT-TALKER, PLUTOCRAT PETE! **HE'LL** STAND UP TO THE REPRESSIVE FORCES OF POLITICAL CORRECTNESS!

ER--YES, WELL--HE **IS** OUTSPOKEN--

--BUT I THINK JEB BUSH WOULD BE A **MUCH** BETTER CANDIDATE--

AH **HA**! SO YOU'RE JUST ANOTHER **FAKE CONSER-VATIVE**! A REPUBLICAN IN **NAME ONLY**!

WELL, DONALD TRUMP DOESN'T **NEED** YOUR MONEY! HE'S GOING TO TAKE THE REPUBLICAN PARTY **BACK**--FROM SELLOUTS LIKE **YOU**!

NOW IF YOU'LL EXCUSE ME, I'VE GOT SOME WHITE PRIDE MEMES TO POST ON SOCIAL MEDIA!

IN FAIRNESS, I SUPPOSE I REALLY SHOULD HAVE SEEN **THAT** COMING.

TOM TOMORROW ©2015

THIS MODERN WORLD

by TOM TOMORROW

Panel 1: DONALD TRUMP MAY HAVE ONE OF THE MOST ELABORATE COMBOVERS IN HISTORY--BUT HE'S VERY PROUD OF THE FACT THAT IT'S HIS REAL HAIR, AND NOT A TOUPEE.

AND IT'S *BIG* HAIR, TOO--THE *BIGGEST!*

ALL THOSE OTHER CANDIDATES ARE SUCH *LOSERS,* WITH THEIR *TINY HAIR!*

Panel 2: IN A WAY, HIS *CAMPAIGN* IS A GIANT, UGLY COMBOVER--A FORM OF ARTIFICE, SOMEHOW PERCEIVED AS MORE "AUTHENTIC" THAN *OTHER* FORMS OF ARTIFICE.

DONALD TRUMP *UNDERSTANDS* ORDINARY AMERICANS--UNLIKE HIS *RIVALS!*

WHAT A BUNCH OF PHONIES *THEY* ARE!

HE WANTS TO MAKE AMERICA *GREAT* AGAIN! IT SAYS SO ON HIS *HAT!*

Panel 3: POLITICAL COMMENTATORS ARE *BAFFLED* BY THE POPULARITY OF THE OPENLY XENOPHOBIC, BLATANTLY MISOGYNISTIC AND PROUDLY UNINFORMED CANDIDATE.

WHAT IS THE SECRET OF HIS APPEAL TO RANK-AND-FILE REPUBLICAN VOTERS?

I'M CERTAINLY STUMPED!

Panel 4: MEANWHILE, THE RULES OF FALSE EQUIVALENCY REQUIRE PUNDITS TO PRETEND THAT TRUMP AND *BERNIE SANDERS* ARE TWO SIDES OF THE SAME COIN.

ONE HAS NO GOVERNING EXPERIENCE WHATSOEVER--WHILE THE OTHER HAS BEEN IN CONGRESS SIXTEEN YEARS!

OTHER THAN THAT-- *TOTALLY* THE SAME!

Panel 5: NOT THAT SANDERS GETS A FRACTION OF TRUMP'S MEDIA COVERAGE.

COMING UP NEXT: DONALD TRUMP SAID *ANOTHER* CRAZY THING!

WE'LL DISCUSS THE CRAZY THING WITH OUR PANEL OF EXPERTS--RIGHT AFTER THIS ANALYSIS OF THE *LAST* CRAZY THING!

IT WAS SURE CRAZY!

Panel 6: IT'S ALL FUN AND GAMES UNTIL THE CRAZY MAN ENDS UP IN THE OVAL OFFICE.

Hey losers and haters! I'm in charge now! So suck on it!

HEH HEH!

Panel 7: AT WHICH POINT, SATIRE BECOMES IRRELEVANT, AND *I* MIGHT AS WELL PACK IT IN.

LOOK AT THIS NICE HAT A LOUD MAN GAVE ME!

TOM TOMORROW ©2015

90

THIS MODERN WORLD

by TOM TOMORROW

PART ONE: THINGS RIGHT-WINGERS FEAR

CHILDREN'S SCIENCE PROJECTS.

HEY--THE KID MADE HIS SO-CALLED "CLOCK" WITH A **CIRCUIT BOARD** AND **WIRES!** IT WAS HALF A BOMB, MINUS THE BOMB PART!

AND HE HAD A **MUSLIM NAME!**

NEED WE SAY MORE?

GAY MARRIAGE.

THE HOMOSEXUALS AND THEIR ENABLERS ARE **IGNORING** WHAT **GOD** WANTS.

OR AT LEAST, WHAT **WE** IMAGINE GOD WANTS!

SAME THING.

SECRET U.S. GOVERNMENT PLANS TO INVADE STATES THAT ARE ALREADY PART OF THE U.S.

OKAY, YES, FALSE ALARM ON THAT WHOLE "JADE HELM" BUSINESS.

OR IS THAT JUST WHAT THEY **WANT** US TO THINK?

DIPLOMACY.

THE IRAN DEAL COULD LEAD TO AN EVEN **DEADLIER** 9/11! DICK CHENEY **SAYS** SO!

AND IF ANYONE SHOULD **KNOW**, IT'S **HIM!**

IMMIGRANTS AND/OR REFUGEES.

THEY'RE CRIMINALS AND TERRORISTS, COMING TO **KILL US ALL!**

WE MIGHT AS WELL JUST BLOW **OURSELVES** UP AND GET IT OVER WITH!

PART TWO: THINGS RIGHT-WINGERS SEE NO NEED TO WORRY ABOUT

MORE THAN 836,000 GUN-RELATED DEATHS SINCE 1989.

EH, THESE THINGS HAPPEN. WHAT CAN YOU DO?

THEY COULD HAVE JUST AS EASILY DIED IN **SWIMMING POOL ACCIDENTS!**

AND OF COURSE: CLIMATE CHANGE.

HA HA! DO WE **LOOK** LIKE PEOPLE WHO SPEND OUR TIME COWERING IN FEAR OF NON-EXISTENT THREATS?

DON'T ANSWER THAT.

TOM TOMORROW ©2015

THIS MODERN WORLD

by TOM TOMORROW

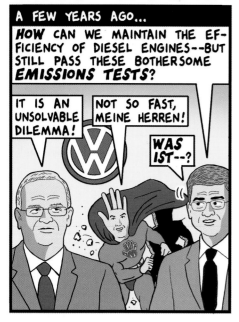

A FEW YEARS AGO...

HOW CAN WE MAINTAIN THE EFFICIENCY OF DIESEL ENGINES--BUT STILL PASS THESE BOTHERSOME **EMISSIONS TESTS?**

IT IS AN UNSOLVABLE DILEMMA!

NOT SO FAST, MEINE HERREN!

WAS IST--?

MEIN GOTT! INVISIBLE HAND OF THE FREE MARKET MAN! BUT--WHY CAN WE **SEE** YOU?

LOOK--IT'S A **METAPHOR!** IT DOES NOT MEAN I AM **LITERALLY INVISIBLE!**

NOW DO YOU WANT MY HELP OR **NOT?** BECAUSE THE ANSWER IS QUITE SIMPLE-- YOU SHOULD **CHEAT!**

JUST HIDE SOME CODE IN THE CAR'S COPYRIGHT-PROTECTED SOFTWARE, INSTRUCTING IT TO TURN ON EMISSION STANDARDS **ONLY** DURING TESTING! PROBLEM **SOLVED!**

WHY--IT'S **BRILLIANT!** IT IS--

--THE GENIUS OF THE FREE MARKET! YES, I KNOW.

AUF WIEDERSEHEN, GENTLEMEN!

MORE RECENTLY...

OH MAN! I BOUGHT THE RIGHTS TO A DRUG USED BY AIDS PATIENTS-- BUT IT ONLY SELLS FOR $13.50 A DOSE! **HOW** AM I SUPPOSED TO MAKE A PROFIT ON **THAT?**

IT'S SIMPLE, SON--RAISE THE PRICE TO **$750** A DOSE!

BUT--WON'T THERE BE A **BACKLASH?**

IT'LL BE **FINE!** THE PUBLIC **LOVES** A SUCCESSFUL ENTREPRENEUR--AND THEY **HATE** GOVERNMENT REGULATION! WHAT COULD GO **WRONG?**

AWE-SOME!

BUT THEN...

I TOOK **YOUR** ADVICE--AND EVERYONE **HATES** ME NOW!

US **TOO!**

ER--

--I'VE NEVER SEEN THOSE LOSERS BEFORE IN MY **LIFE!** THEY'RE JUST SOME **BAD APPLES**--WHO SHOULD **DEFINITELY** NOT UNDERMINE YOUR FAITH IN THE **FREE MARKET!**

HA HA! AS **IF!**

? !

NEXT TIME...

THE AMERICAN PEOPLE **LOVE** A WINNER, DONALD!

THE FREE MARKET HAS **SPOKEN!**

TOM TOMORROW ©2015

THIS MODERN WORLD

by TOM TOMORROW

Panel 1: HOLOGRAPHIC TEACHING INTERFACE *ACTIVATED!* GOOD MORNING, CHILDREN! IT'S TIME TO RESUME OUR STUDY OF YOUR 21ST CENTURY ANCESTORS--KNOWN TO HISTORIANS AS THE *WANKIEST GENERATION!*

Panel 2: IN *THOSE* DAYS, CHILDREN SUCH AS YOURSELVES GATHERED TOGETHER PHYSICALLY IN *PUBLIC CLASSROOMS!* OF COURSE, THE RELENTLESS EPIDEMIC OF GUN RAMPAGES ABOUT WHICH NOTHING COULD BE DONE PUT AN END TO *THAT!*

Panel 3: THAT'S WHY *YOU* CHILDREN ARE SECURE IN YOUR INDIVIDUAL *CONTAINMENT PODS*, DEEP IN YOUR FAMILY *BUNKERS!*

GIVEN THE SACROSANCT INVIOLABILITY OF *GUN RIGHTS*, IT WAS THE BEST SOLUTION ADULTS WERE ABLE TO DEVISE.

Panel 4: INCIDENTALLY, THERE HAVE BEEN 17 ROUTINE GUN-RELATED MASS FATALITY EVENTS IN THE LAST 48 MINUTES. AS ALWAYS, EXERCISE CAUTION WHEN VENTURING *OUTSIDE* OF YOUR BUNKERS!

Panel 5: SPEAKING OF BUNKERS--DID YOU KNOW YOUR ANCESTORS MOVED ABOUT FREELY ON THE PLANET'S *SURFACE*--BEFORE CONSTANT RAGING HELLSTORMS FORCED THE HUMAN RACE TO SEEK SHELTER *UNDERGROUND?*

WHY, THEY DIDN'T EVEN HAVE TO RECYCLE THEIR OWN *URINE* BACK THEN!

Panel 6: GOVERNMENT DEVOLVED INTO DYSFUNCTIONAL CHAOS IN THOSE YEARS-- THANKS LARGELY TO "TEA PARTY" POLITICIANS WHO HAD BEEN ELECTED TO GOVERN ON THE BASIS OF THEIR *HATRED* OF GOVERNMENT.

YOU'D THINK YOUR ANCESTORS WOULD HAVE SEEN *THAT* ONE COMING.

Panel 7: THESE LEADERS WERE WILLING TO SHUT THE GOVERNMENT DOWN *ENTIRELY*--AND RISK PLUNGING THE ECONOMY INTO A MAJOR DEPRESSION--

Panel 8: --IN ORDER TO DEFUND AN ORGANIZATION DEVOTED TO *REPRODUCTIVE HEALTH CARE!*

AS AN ARTIFICIAL INTELLIGENCE SUBROUTINE, I AM UNABLE TO EXPLAIN THEIR OBSESSIVE HOSTILITY TO THIS BASIC FUNCTION OF BIOLOGICAL EXISTENCE.

Panel 9: WELL, THAT'S ALL THE BANDWIDTH WE'VE BEEN ALLOCATED FOR TODAY! TOMORROW, WE'LL TAKE A LOOK AT THE LEGENDARY PRESIDENTIAL RACE OF 2016--AND THE ELECTION OF *PERMANENT PRESIDENT TRUMP'S BRAIN*--

--BACK WHEN IT STILL HAD A *PHYSICAL BODY!*

BUH-*BYE!*

THIS MODERN WORLD

by TOM TOMORROW

DRONEY, YOU KEEP TELLING US THAT DRONE STRIKES ARE *SURGICALLY PRECISE!*

BUT ACCORDING TO A BIG REPORT IN *THE INTERCEPT*, 90% OF PEOPLE KILLED BY DRONES IN ONE FIVE MONTH PERIOD IN AFGHANISTAN WERE *NOT* THE *INTENDED TARGETS!*

OF COURSE, THE NUMBER OF UNINTENTIONAL DRONE CASUALTIES IS OBSCURED BECAUSE THE MILITARY ROUTINELY CLASSIFIES UNIDENTIFIED VICTIMS AS *"ENEMIES KILLED IN ACTION"!*

WELL, TO PARAPHRASE AN OLD SAYING--

"--THERE ARE NO *STRANGERS*, ONLY ENEMIES I HAVEN'T *KILLED* YET!"

NO?

SIGH.

NO ONE APPRECIATES MY DRY SENSE OF HUMOR.

BUT SERIOUSLY, I KEEP TRYING TO TELL YOU KIDS--ACCIDENTS *HAPPEN!* AND NOT JUST WITH *DRONES!*

LIKE WHEN THAT AC-130 GUNSHIP ACCIDENTALLY BOMBED THE HELL OUT OF THAT *HOSPITAL* IT, UM, DELIBERATELY TARGETED.

PROBABLY NOT THE BEST EXAMPLE, NOW THAT I THINK ABOUT IT.

LOOK AT IT THIS WAY--I'M A *DISRUPTIVE INNOVATOR*, RE-IMAGINING WAR ITSELF! I REPRESENT A *NEW PARADIGM!*

THE OLD RULES DON'T *APPLY* TO *ME!*

IF BY "NEW PARADIGM" YOU MEAN "EXTRAJUDICIAL ASSASSINATION PROGRAM THAT FREQUENTLY KILLS BYSTANDERS."

A.K.A. WORST STARTUP *EVER.*

LUDDITES.

TOM TOMORROW ©2015

94

THIS MODERN WORLD

by TOM TOMORROW

THERE IS NO ESCAPE FROM...

THE CAMPAIGN SEASON OF THE DAMNED

BWAH HA HA HA HA HA!

FOOLISH MORTAL VOTERS! DO YOU THINK YOU CAN WITHSTAND THE ENDLESS TORMENT OF THE *PERPETUAL CAMPAIGN?*

CANADA'S ELECTION LASTED ELEVEN WEEKS, START TO FINISH!

THAT WON'T EVEN GET *US* TO THE *IOWA CAUCUSES!*

CAN YOU ENDURE THE TERRIFYING CACOPHONY OF *DEMOCRATS WHO SUPPORT RIVAL CANDIDATES?*

YOOUUU... ARE A BERNIE-BRO....!

YOOUUU... ARE A HILLARY-BOT....!

WILL THE HORROR OF THE *REPUBLICAN* FIELD PERVADE YOUR VERY *SOUL?*

THE JEWS SHOULD HAVE PREVENTED THE HOLOCAUST!

GLOBAL WARMING IS A HOAX!

LIBERALS WANT TO HARVEST BABY BRAINS!

DOES THE POSSIBILITY OF *PRESIDENT TRUMP* FILL YOU WITH BONE-CHILLING *DREAD?*

WE'RE DOING THINGS MY WAY NOW, LOSERS AND HATERS!

NOOO!

WILL YOU SURVIVE THE DESCENT INTO REALITY-WARPING MADNESS WITH YOUR OWN SANITY *INTACT?*

YOU REMEMBER HOW MY BROTHER KEPT US *SAFE*, DON'T YOU?

DON'T YOU?

BUT I--I *DON'T* REMEMBER THAT...

AND AS SOON AS *THIS* ELECTION IS OVER...WE'LL GET STARTED ON THE *NEXT* ONE!

TOM TOMORROW©2015

THIS MODERN WORLD

by TOM TOMORROW

PART ONE: IN WHICH WINGNUTS DISCUSS THE RIGHT TO KEEP AND BEAR ARMS

THE ONLY THING STOPPING A POTENTIAL TYRANT LIKE OBAMA FROM SENDING ALL HIS OPPONENTS TO *FEMA* CAMPS--

--IS THE KNOWLEDGE THAT CITIZEN PATRIOTS SUCH AS OURSELVES ARE ARMED AND READY TO FIGHT *BACK!*

THAT'S WHY WE STAND WITH *CLIVEN BUNDY*--AND ANYONE ELSE WHO REFUSES TO BACK DOWN IN THE FACE OF GOVERNMENT OVERREACH!

JUST BECAUSE SOMEONE IS WEARING A *UNIFORM*-- IT DOESN'T MEAN THEY'RE ENTITLED TO UNQUESTIONING *OBEDIENCE!*

THIS IS *AMERICA*, AFTER ALL! WE ARE NOT SHEEPLE, MINDLESSLY SUBMITTING TO SOME FUNCTIONARY WITH A *BADGE!*

WE ARE PREPARED TO DO *WHATEVER* IT TAKES TO DEFEND OUR GOD-GIVEN LIBERTY FROM THE CAPRICIOUS ABUSE OF POWER!

PART TWO: IN WHICH THEY DISCUSS THE BLACK TEENAGER MANHANDLED BY A SCHOOL COP IN SOUTH CAROLINA

HEY, SHE DISOBEYED A POLICE OFFICER'S DIRECT COMMAND! WHAT DID SHE *EXPECT?*

SOME PEOPLE HAVE *NO* RESPECT FOR LAW AND ORDER! IF YOU KNOW WHO WE MEAN.

AND WE THINK YOU DO.

NEXT: HELLO, FELLOW GUN ENTHUSIASTS!

EEK! CALL THE *POLICE!*

TOM TOMORROW ©2015

THIS MODERN WORLD
by TOM TOMORROW

G.O.P. DREAM DEBATE

THE MODERATORS

A RIGHT-WING NUTCASE
YARGLE BARGLE

AND ANOTHER
BLARGH!

AND ONE MORE

THE QUESTIONS

MR. TRUMP, DO YOU TAKE YOUR COFFEE WITH CREAM AND/OR SUGAR?

DR. CARSON, HAVE YOU SEEN ANY GOOD MOVIES LATELY?

MS. FIORINA, WHAT IS YOUR FAVORITE COLOR?

SENATOR RUBIO, IF YOU WERE A TREE, WHAT KIND OF TREE WOULD YOU BE?

SENATOR CRUZ, WOULD YOU AGREE THAT TINY KITTENS ARE UTTERLY ADORABLE?

GOVERNOR BUSH, WASSUP?

IN CLOSING, WOULD YOU EACH PLEASE RANT ABOUT HILLARY CLINTON AND BENGHAZI FOR THIRTY SECONDS.

THE POST-DEBATE RITUAL

ENOUGH WITH ALL THESE "*GOTCHA*" QUESTIONS!

WHAT *WAS* THAT-- THE SPANISH *IN-QUISITION*?

?!

AND THEN

THE *NEXT* DEBATE SHOULD BE MODERATED BY A PANEL OF AUDIO-ANIMATRONIC *REAGAN ROBOTS!*

BUT LATER

WHO *PRO-GRAMMED* THOSE ROBOTS?

TOM TOMORROW ©2015

THIS MODERN WORLD

by TOM TOMORROW

SIZZLING HOT TAKES

BECAUSE PARIS WAS ATTACKED BY *TERRORISTS*--

--AMERICAN COLLEGE STUDENTS HAVE NO RIGHT TO COMPLAIN ABOUT *RACISM!*

THE ONLY THING THAT CAN STOP BAD GUYS WITH GUNS IS FOR EVERY SINGLE PERSON ON THE PLANET TO CARRY A GUN AT ALL TIMES.

A HEAVILY ARMED GLOBAL POPULATION IS A *POLITE* GLOBAL POPULATION!

OBVIOUSLY WE MUST KEEP GITMO OPEN--REMOVE ANY RESTRICTIONS ON THE N.S.A.--AND SEND LARGE NUMBERS OF TROOPS TO IRAQ AND SYRIA AND *KEEP* THEM THERE!

IT WILL *TOTALLY* WORK OUT *THIS* TIME!

THIS TRAGEDY CLEARLY DEMONSTRATES WHY EVERYONE SHOULD EMBRACE *MY* OPINION ON AN *ENTIRELY UNRELATED TOPIC!*

OOH! MINE *TOO!*

AND *MINE!*

IN SUCH A DANGEROUS WORLD, AMERICA *NEEDS* THE STRONG, DECISIVE, LEVEL-HEADED LEADER-SHIP...OF *DONALD TRUMP!*

OR PERHAPS BEN CARSON.

WHAT COULD GO WRONG?

GRIT YOUR TEETH AND ACT LIKE YOU BELIEVE IT.

DOING MY BEST.

TOM TOMORROW ©2015

THIS MODERN WORLD

by TOM TOMORROW

HOME OF THE BRAVE

THE ATTACKS IN FRANCE WERE ALSO AN ASSAULT ON **OUR** MOST CHERISHED VALUES--

--WHICH WE ARE PREPARED TO JETTISON AT A MOMENT'S NOTICE!

MANY AMERICANS FOCUSED THEIR INCHOATE FEAR OF TERRORISM ON THE MENACE OF REFUGEES **FLEEING** TERRORISM.

WE SHOULDN'T EVEN BE ACCEPTING ORPHANED **TODDLERS!**

THEY **COULD** BE VERY SMALL TERRORISTS IN **DISGUISE!**

WE CAN'T TAKE **ANY CHANCES** AT A TIME LIKE **THIS!**

ONE TEXAS LAWMAKER OPENLY WORRIED THAT HIS STATE'S LAX GUN LAWS WOULD MAKE IT TOO EASY FOR REFUGEES TO PROCURE FIREARMS.

CAN YOU **IMAGINE** WHAT COULD HAPPEN--IF PEOPLE OF ILL INTENT HAD READY ACCESS TO SUCH WEAPONRY?

HORRIFIC GUN MASSACRES COULD BECOME A **ROUTINE OCCURRENCE!**

AND OF COURSE THERE'S THE SUGGESTION (EMBRACED BY JEB BUSH) THAT WE SHOULD ONLY ADMIT "PROVEN CHRISTIANS"...

BUT--WHAT IF THEY'RE REALLY SECRET **MUSLIMS?**

WE COULD MAKE THEM TAKE SOME SORT OF **BIBLE QUIZ!**

AND ALSO MAKE SURE THEY HATE GAY MARRIAGE AND STUFF.

JOHN KASICH PROPOSED "PAUSING" REFUGEE RELOCATION--AND CREATING A PROPAGANDA BUREAU TO SPREAD "JUDEO-CHRISTIAN VALUES."

LOOK **OUT**, REFUGEES WHO MIGHT BE TERRORISTS! **ASS-KICKING AMERICAN JESUS** IS HERE!

YOU WANT INTO **MY** COUNTRY--

--YOU GOTTA GET PAST **ME.**

A DRAMATIZATION FROM THE UNITED STATES DEPARTMENT OF APPROVED RELIGIONS

MEANWHILE THE AMERICAN RIGHT STANDS IN SOLIDARITY WITH FRANCE-- JUST LIKE THEY **ALWAYS** HAVE!

WHEN WE USED TO CALL THEM "CHEESE-EATING SURRENDER MONKEYS"--

--WE MEANT IT IN THE **BEST POSSIBLE WAY!**

NOW LET'S GO EAT SOME **FREEDOM FRIES!**

TOM TOMORROW ©2015

99

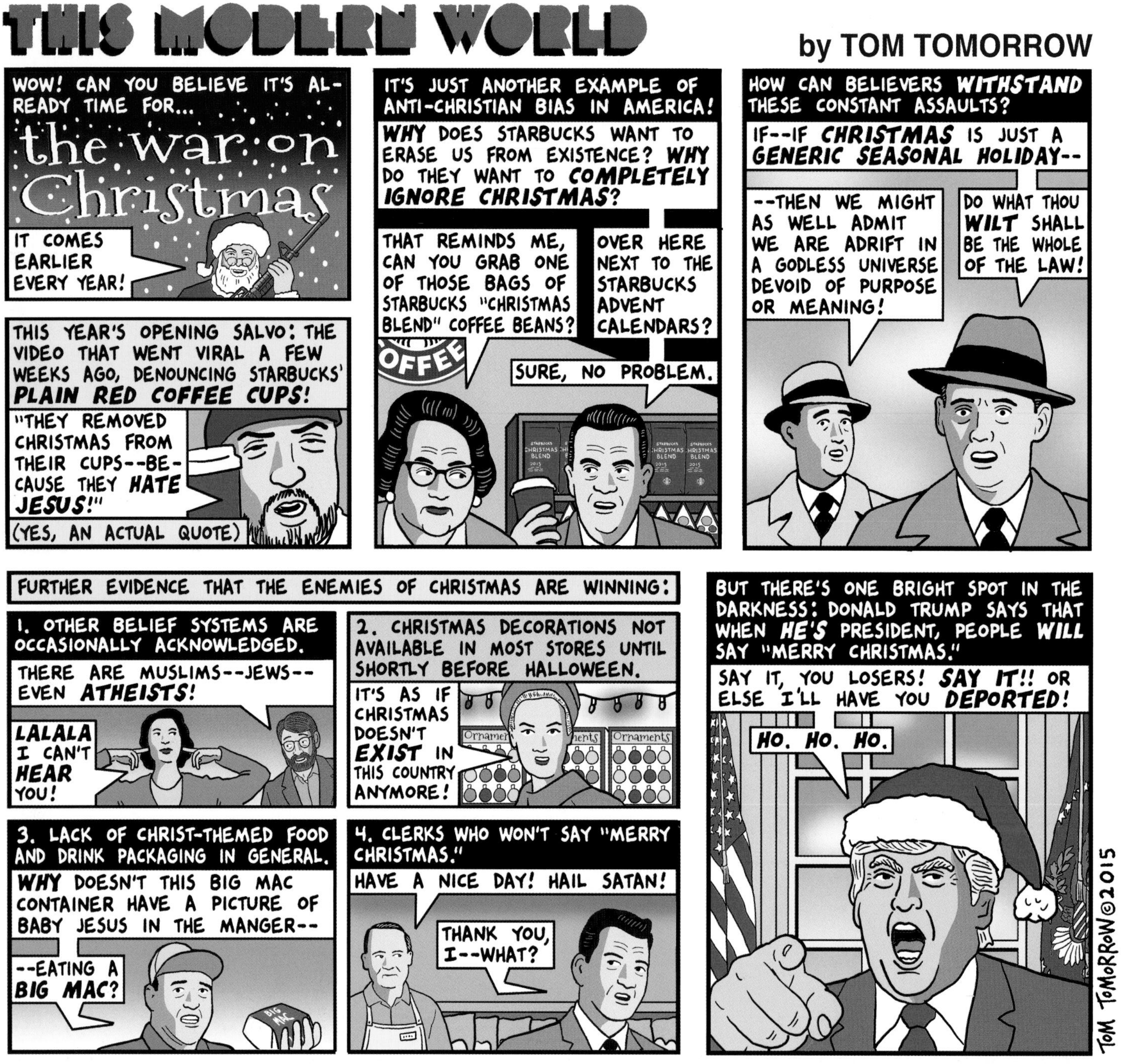
THIS MODERN WORLD
by TOM TOMORROW
WOW! CAN YOU BELIEVE IT'S ALREADY TIME FOR...
the war on Christmas
IT COMES EARLIER EVERY YEAR!
THIS YEAR'S OPENING SALVO: THE VIDEO THAT WENT VIRAL A FEW WEEKS AGO, DENOUNCING STARBUCKS' PLAIN RED COFFEE CUPS!
"THEY REMOVED CHRISTMAS FROM THEIR CUPS--BECAUSE THEY HATE JESUS!"
(YES, AN ACTUAL QUOTE)
IT'S JUST ANOTHER EXAMPLE OF ANTI-CHRISTIAN BIAS IN AMERICA!
WHY DOES STARBUCKS WANT TO ERASE US FROM EXISTENCE? WHY DO THEY WANT TO COMPLETELY IGNORE CHRISTMAS?
THAT REMINDS ME, CAN YOU GRAB ONE OF THOSE BAGS OF STARBUCKS "CHRISTMAS BLEND" COFFEE BEANS?
OVER HERE NEXT TO THE STARBUCKS ADVENT CALENDARS?
SURE, NO PROBLEM.
COFFEE
HOW CAN BELIEVERS WITHSTAND THESE CONSTANT ASSAULTS?
IF--IF CHRISTMAS IS JUST A GENERIC SEASONAL HOLIDAY--
--THEN WE MIGHT AS WELL ADMIT WE ARE ADRIFT IN A GODLESS UNIVERSE DEVOID OF PURPOSE OR MEANING!
DO WHAT THOU WILT SHALL BE THE WHOLE OF THE LAW!
FURTHER EVIDENCE THAT THE ENEMIES OF CHRISTMAS ARE WINNING:
1. OTHER BELIEF SYSTEMS ARE OCCASIONALLY ACKNOWLEDGED.
THERE ARE MUSLIMS--JEWS--EVEN ATHEISTS!
LALALA I CAN'T HEAR YOU!
2. CHRISTMAS DECORATIONS NOT AVAILABLE IN MOST STORES UNTIL SHORTLY BEFORE HALLOWEEN.
IT'S AS IF CHRISTMAS DOESN'T EXIST IN THIS COUNTRY ANYMORE!
Ornaments
3. LACK OF CHRIST-THEMED FOOD AND DRINK PACKAGING IN GENERAL.
WHY DOESN'T THIS BIG MAC CONTAINER HAVE A PICTURE OF BABY JESUS IN THE MANGER--
--EATING A BIG MAC?
BIG MAC
4. CLERKS WHO WON'T SAY "MERRY CHRISTMAS."
HAVE A NICE DAY! HAIL SATAN!
THANK YOU, I--WHAT?
BUT THERE'S ONE BRIGHT SPOT IN THE DARKNESS: DONALD TRUMP SAYS THAT WHEN HE'S PRESIDENT, PEOPLE WILL SAY "MERRY CHRISTMAS."
SAY IT, YOU LOSERS! SAY IT!! OR ELSE I'LL HAVE YOU DEPORTED!
HO. HO. HO.
TOM TOMORROW©2015

THIS MODERN WORLD

by TOM TOMORROW

WELL, HERE WE ARE IN YET ANOTHER GUN MASSACRE CARTOON.

YES, BUT THIS TIME IT'S *DIFFERENT*--THE SHOOTERS WERE *MUSLIM!*

WE HAVE TO CLOSE ALL THE MOSQUES! REGISTER ALL MUSLIMS! INCREASE DOMESTIC SURVEILLANCE! DEPORT AS MANY OF THEM AS WE *CAN!*

AND JUST FOR GOOD MEASURE, LET'S GET SOME TROOPS ON THE GROUND IN, UM, SYRIA. OR WHEREVER.

BUT NO GUN CONTROL, I TAKE IT?

GOOD LORD, OF COURSE NOT! *THAT* WILL NEVER WORK! WE HAVE TO FOCUS ON *PRACTICAL* SOLUTIONS!

BY WHICH YOU MEAN MASS DEPORTATIONS AND ENDLESS WAR.

A GIANT WALL ALONG THE BORDER WOULDN'T HURT, EITHER.

TOM TOMORROW ©2015

THIS MODERN WORLD

by TOM TOMORROW

2015 IN REVIEW

IN WHICH WE BARELY SCRATCH THE SURFACE OF THE YEAR IN CRAZY

PART THE SECOND

JULY 9: TRUMP SAYS HE STILL DOES NOT KNOW IF OBAMA WAS BORN IN U.S.

BECAUSE I AM A RATIONAL PERSON WHO THINKS VERY RATIONAL THINGS!

AUG. 8: TRUMP SAYS DEBATE HOST MEGYN KELLY HAD "BLOOD COMING OUT OF HER WHEREVER"; PUNDITS PREDICT END OF HIS CAMPAIGN.

THIS TIME HE HAS GONE TOO FAR!

THEY ARE, OF COURSE, WRONG.

AUG. 25: TRUMP SUPPORTER FAMOUSLY DECLARES:

"HIS GOAL IS TO MAKE AMERICA GREAT AGAIN! IT'S ON HIS HAT!"

NEITHER TRUMP NOR SUPPORTERS SPECIFY WHEN IT WAS GREAT THE FIRST TIME.

SEPT. 3: KENTUCKY MARRIAGE LICENSE CLERK HEADS TO JAIL FOR FIVE DAYS RATHER THAN ISSUE LICENSES TO GAY COUPLES.

SHE'S JUST LIKE ROSA PARKS, EXCEPT THE OPPOSITE!

SEPT. 17: JEB BUSH DECLARES THAT HIS BROTHER KEPT US SAFE.

IF BY "SAFE" YOU MEAN--

--OH, WHY DO I EVEN BOTHER?

SEPT. 18: CARLY FIORINA DENOUNCES IMAGINARY PLANNED PARENTHOOD VIDEO.

--AND THEN THEY TAKE BABY BRAINS AND FEED THEM TO ZOMBIES!

I'VE SEEN THE FOOTAGE!

OCT. 2: JEB BLURS LINE BETWEEN REALITY AND SATIRICAL CARTOONS, RESPONDS TO LATEST MASS SHOOTING:

"STUFF HAPPENS!"

SERIOUSLY, THIS IS WHAT HE SAID.

OCT. 9: BEN CARSON SAYS JEWS COULD HAVE PREVENTED HOLOCAUST WITH GUNS.

BECAUSE I AM ALSO A VERY RATIONAL PERSON!

THE G.O.P. IS FULL OF THEM!

OCT. 13: HILLARY CLINTON SAYS EDWARD SNOWDEN SHOULD HAVE STAYED IN U.S. AS WHISTLEBLOWER.

THEN WE COULD HAVE IGNORED HIS REVELATIONS AND PROSECUTED HIM!

THE SYSTEM WORKS!

OCT. 28: MIKE HUCKABEE OFFERS HIS VERSION OF HEALTH CARE REFORM.

"LET'S CURE... DIABETES, HEART DISEASE, CANCER AND ALZHEIMERS!"

GRATEFUL NATION WONDERS WHY NO ONE THOUGHT OF THIS BEFORE.

NOV. 9: WEIGHING IN ON IMPORTANT DEBATE, JEB BUSH DECLARES:

HELL YEAH I'D KILL BABY HITLER!

IN RESPONSE TO PRANK QUESTION, BEN CARSON LATER SAYS HE WOULD NOT ABORT BABY HITLER.

NOV. 13: TERRORISTS ATTACK PARIS, CAUSING MANY AMERICANS TO IMMEDIATELY FORGET THE LAST 13 YEARS.

BOMB THEM! INVADE THEM!

WHAT COULD GO WRONG?

MID-NOVEMBER: AS CHRISTMAS APPROACHES, IRONY-IMMUNE RIGHT-WINGERS INSIST DESPERATE MIDDLE EASTERN REFUGEES BE DENIED SANCTUARY.

TRY CANADA.

NOV. 19: WHISTLEBLOWER SAYS U.S. DRONE OPERATORS REFER TO CHILDREN AS "FUN-SIZE TERRORISTS."

AND THERE'S NOT MUCH WE CAN ADD TO THAT.

NOV. 27: CONSERVATIVES SHRUG OFF ANOTHER WHITE GUY GUN RAMPAGE.

NOTHING CAN BE DONE!

DEC. 2: CONSERVATIVES ARE VERY ALARMED BY MUSLIM GUN RAMPAGE.

SOMETHING MUST BE DONE!

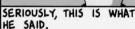

DEC. 7: TRUMP EMBRACES HIS INNER FASCIST.

BAN ALL MUSLIMS! SHUT DOWN THE MOSQUES!

EIN REICH! EIN VOLK!

HIS POLL NUMBERS GO UP.

DEC 14: TRUMP'S DOCTOR RELEASES EXTREMELY CONVINCING LETTER OF MEDICAL FITNESS.

"MR. TRUMP... WILL BE THE HEALTHIEST INDIVIDUAL EVER ELECTED TO THE PRESIDENCY!"

DEC. 15: TED CRUZ EXPLAINS HIS PLAN TO DEFEAT ISIS.

"WE NEED TO FOCUS ON KILLING THE BAD GUYS!"

GRATEFUL NATION WONDERS WHY NO ONE THOUGHT OF THIS BEFORE.

NEXT YEAR: MORE GUN MASSACRES! MORE WAR! AND MORE DONALD TRUMP!

SO--LIKE THIS YEAR--

--ONLY MORE!

TOM TOMORROW ©2015 • APOLOGIES TO MATT GROENING

THIS MODERN WORLD
by TOM TOMORROW

2015 IN REVIEW

A HIGHLY SUBJECTIVE AND INHERENTLY INCOMPLETE LOOK BACK AT THE YEAR THAT WAS

PART THE FIRST

JAN. 7: FIVE CARTOONISTS (AND SEVEN OTHERS) DIE IN CHARLIE HEBDO MASSACRE, SETTING OFF INTENSE SOCIAL MEDIA DEBATE ABOUT HOW OFFENSIVE THEIR CARTOONS WERE.

SIGH.

JAN. 26: IN LEGISLATIVE MANEUVER, SENATE GOP VOTES TO CONFIRM THAT CLIMATE CHANGE IS REAL (BUT NOT MANMADE).

VOTE IS QUICKLY FORGOTTEN.

HEY AL GORE! IT'S *SNOWING* AGAIN! HAW HAW HAW!

FEB. 9: IOWA REP. STEVE KING CALLS OBAMA SPEECH A "JIHADI RECRUITMENT TOOL."

AND I POSTED A CARTOON OF OBAMA IN A *TURBAN*!

BECAUSE I AM A VERY SERIOUS PERSON.

FEB. 11: TWELVE YEARS AFTER THE START OF THE WAR, SOMEONE FINALLY FACES CONSEQUENCES FOR LYING ABOUT IRAQ.

--AND THEN MY CHOPPER TOOK A *DI-RECT HIT*!

UNFORTUNATELY IT'S THIS GUY.

FEB. 11: STUDY FINDS U.S. HAS MORE GUN DEATHS THAN ANY OTHER DEVELOPED NATION.

THERE'S ONLY ONE SOLUTION--

--*MORE GUNS*!

FEB. 19: MOTHER JONES DEBUNKS BILL O'REILLY'S CLAIM THAT HE "EXPERIENCED COMBAT."

I WAS IN THE *MIDDLE* OF THE FALKLANDS WAR!

OR AT LEAST IN THE SAME *HEMISPHERE*!

MARCH 5: DINESH D'SOUZA SAYS HILLARY CLINTON AND OBAMA THINK THEY'RE ABOVE THE LAW.

HE MAKES THIS STATEMENT VIA SKYPE FROM THE COMMUNITY CONFINEMENT CENTER WHERE HE IS SERVING AN EIGHT MONTH SENTENCE FOR VIOLATING CAMPAIGN FINANCE LAWS.

MARCH 16: McDONALDS SUED FOR TELLING WORKERS TO PUT MUSTARD AND MAYONNAISE ON BURNS.

ADD SOME SECRET SAUCE AND YOU'LL BE *DELICIOUS*!

WHAT?

APRIL 2: SEN. COTTON POINTS OUT THAT "IN IRAN, THEY *HANG* YOU... FOR BEING GAY!"

UNLESS YOU'RE LITERALLY SUBJECT TO THE *DEATH PENALTY*--

--YOU HAVE *NOTHING* TO COMPLAIN ABOUT!

APRIL 8: COTTON REMAINS ON A ROLL, DECLARING WAR WITH IRAN WOULD ONLY TAKE A FEW DAYS.

IT'LL BE A *CAKEWALK*!

WHY ARE YOU LOOKING AT ME LIKE THAT?

APRIL 23: AFTER TWO WESTERN HOSTAGES ARE KILLED IN DRONE STRIKES, U.S. ADMITS IT DIDN'T KNOW WHO IT WAS TARGETING.

IT JUST DEPENDS ON WHAT THE MEANING OF "NEAR CERTAINTY" IS.

APRIL 29: QUOTING ANONYMOUS POLICE DOCUMENT, WASH. POST INITIALLY REPORTS THAT FREDDIE GRAY CAUSED OWN INJURIES.

HE WAS SO DEVIOUS-- HE SEVERED HIS *OWN SPINE*!

MAY 21: JEB BUSH SAYS BROTHER MISLED INTO WAR BY "BAD INTELLIGENCE."

YOU MEAN, HIS *OWN*?

NO THAT IS NOT WHAT I MEAN.

MAY 28: 62% OF REPUBLICANS STILL THINK IRAQ WAR WAS GOOD DECISION.

HOW *ELSE* WOULD WE HAVE DESTABILIZED THE MIDDLE EAST AND CREATED A STATE OF PERMANENT WAR?

ANSWER *THAT*, LIBTARDS!

JUNE 2: TSA SCREENERS FAIL TO DETECT WEAPONS AND EXPLOSIVES IN 67 OF 70 TESTS.

BUT WE'RE *TOTALLY* AWESOME AT CONFISCATING *SHAMPOO*!

JUNE 16: DONALD TRUMP LAUNCHES WHAT MANY ASSUME WILL BE AN EXTREMELY SHORT-LIVED PRESIDENTIAL CAMPAIGN.

MEXICANS ARE DRUG SMUGGLING *RAPISTS*!

LITTLE DID WE KNOW.

JUNE 19: RACIST CHARLESTON SHOOTER LEADS WALL ST. JOURNAL TO DECLARE "INSTITUTIONAL RACISM" OVER.

THE MURDERS WERE WIDELY CONDEMNED--AND POLICE ARRESTED THE GUNMAN!

(THIS WAS REALLY THEIR ARGUMENT.)

JUNE 25: SCOTUS UPHOLDS OBAMACARE.

JUNE 26: SCOTUS UPHOLDS GAY MARRIAGE.

JUNE 27: AMERICA NOT DESTROYED BY ANGRY RIGHT-WING GOD.

YET.

HMMPH.

JUNE 29: TRUMP PROMISES TO CHANGE HAIRSTYLE IF ELECTED PRESIDENT.

I'LL SAVE *HOURS* A DAY!

AND I'LL *USE* THOSE HOURS--TO MAKE AMERICA *GREAT* AGAIN!

TOM TOMORROW ©2015

103

THIS MODERN WORLD

by TOM TOMORROW

WELCOME TO THE MIND-BENDING REALM OF...

THE QUANTUM REPUBLICAN UNIVERSE

IN THE QUANTUM REPUBLICAN UNIVERSE, REALITY IS EXTREMELY MALLEABLE.

MAYBE THE PLANNED PARENTHOOD SHOOTER WAS A *TRANSGENDERED LIBERAL ACTIVIST!*

I'VE *SEEN* THE BABY-HARVESTING VIDEOS! *I'VE SEEN THEM!*

THE PYRAMIDS ARE *GRAIN SILOS!* DEFINITELY NOT BUILT BY ALIENS, THOUGH.

IN THIS STRANGE DOMAIN, THE TRADITIONAL LAWS OF CAUSE AND EFFECT NO LONGER *APPLY!*

THE EASY AVAILABILITY OF GUNS IN THIS COUNTRY HAD *NOTHING* TO DO WITH THE MOST RECENT GUN MASSACRE!

OR THE ONE BEFORE THAT!

OR THE ONE BEFORE THAT!

OR THE ONE BEFORE *THAT!*

THINGS ARE TRUE HERE BECAUSE QUANTUM REPUBLICANS *WANT* THEM TO BE TRUE.

GLOBAL WARMING IS A LIBERAL *HOAX!*

TAX CUTS FOR THE *RICH* BENEFIT *EVERYONE!*

BANNING ALL MUSLIMS IS SO CONSTITUTIONAL, IT WILL MAKE YOUR *HEAD* SPIN!

SOME INHABITANTS ARE ABLE TO CONSTRUCT *ENTIRELY* SELF-CONTAINED REALITIES--THROUGH THE SHEER POWER OF THEIR *VERBIAGE!*

I SAW *THOUSANDS* OF MUSLIMS HAVING A GREAT BIG DANCE PARTY ON SEPTEMBER 11! I HAVE AN *AMAZING* MEMORY--THE *BEST!* IF YOU CAN'T FIND THE VIDEOS, THEY MUST HAVE BEEN *ERASED!*

WHO YOU GONNA BELIEVE-- *ME,* OR ALL THE LOSERS WHO *AREN'T* ME?

OBSERVERS *OUTSIDE* THE QUANTUM REPUBLICAN UNIVERSE APPEAR TO HAVE *NO* IMPACT ON THE PHENOMENON BEING OBSERVED.

WE DON'T CARE WHAT THE BIASED MEDIA SAY ABOUT DONALD TRUMP!

THEY'RE ALL *LOSERS* WHO SHOULD BE FIRED ANYWAY!

MR. TRUMP *SAID* SO!

WILL IT CONTINUE TO EXPAND--AND ENGULF US *ALL?* STAY *TUNED!*

TOM TOMORROW ©2015

THIS MODERN WORLD

by TOM TOMORROW

Panel 1:

Hey kids! It's time for a peek into...

The Awesome World of THE FUTURE!

Featuring noted futurologist Dr. Wilbur von Philbert

© 1978 Educational Films Inc.

GREETINGS, CHILDREN! LET'S GET *STARTED!*

Panel 2:

IN THE *FUTURE*, OUR LEADERS WILL BE CAREFULLY CHOSEN FOR THEIR *WISDOM* AND *MATURITY!*

I MUST DEFER TO MY ESTEEMED OPPONENT, WHOSE GOVERNING EXPERIENCE FAR SURPASSES MY OWN!

NONSENSE! *MY* OPPONENT IS A HUMBLE MAN OF *IMPRESSIVE* INTELLECTUAL DEPTH!

RUBIO FOR LEADER

TRUMP FOR LEADER

Panel 3:

OUR POLITICAL DISCOURSE WILL BE THOUGHTFUL AND RATIONAL.

IT'S HARD TO BELIEVE THERE WERE ONCE PRESIDENTIAL CANDIDATES WHO PROUDLY *EMBRACED* IGNORANCE, RESENTMENT, AND XENOPHOBIA!

SUCH BARBARIC ATTITUDES ARE *LITERALLY* INCOMPREHENSIBLE TO THE MODERN MIND!

Panel 4:

PREJUDICE AND INTOLERANCE WILL BE NOTHING BUT DISTANT MEMORIES FROM A LESS ENLIGHTENED ERA.

OUR *ANCESTORS* WERE BESET BY HATRED INEXPLICABLY BASED ON SKIN COLOR, SEXUAL ORIENTATION, AND VARIOUS TRIBAL AFFILIATIONS!

FORTUNATELY THEIR PRIMITIVE ANIMOSITY DID NOT SURVIVE INTO *THIS* DAY AND AGE!

Panel 5:

AND OF COURSE, MISOGYNY AND SEXISM WILL SIMILARLY BE LONG FORGOTTEN.

HOW COULD ANYONE POSSIBLY TREAT ANOTHER HUMAN BEING AS LESS THAN EQUAL, BASED SOLELY ON THE CONFIGURATION OF THEIR *REPRODUCTIVE ORGANS*?

THE STRANGERS WITH WHOM I CONVERSE ON THE GLOBAL COMPUTER NETWORK FIND IT *UTTERLY* PERPLEXING!

Panel 6:

WOW! HOW SOON WILL THIS INCREDIBLE WORLD *ARRIVE*, DR. VON PHILBERT?

OH, I'D SAY BY JANUARY 2016 AT THE *LATEST!*

IF WE HAVEN'T FIGURED THINGS OUT BY *THEN*, WE MIGHT AS WELL *GIVE UP!*

I MEAN, WHAT *ELSE* ARE WE GOING TO USE OUR FUTURE BRAINS FOR--*DATING APPS?*

UM--WHAT'S AN "APP"?

TOM TOMORROW © 2016

THIS MODERN WORLD

by TOM TOMORROW

HEY KIDS! IT'S THE ALL NEW

JUNIOR MILITIAMAN ANTI-GOVERNMENT PLAYSET

COMES COMPLETE WITH **REAL WORKING FIREARMS!***

LOOK OUT, EVERYONE! I'M A **GOOD GUY WITH A GUN!**

AT LEAST, UNTIL SOMEBODY DOES SOMETHING I DON'T **LIKE!**

*WARNING: EXERCISE OF SECOND AMENDMENT RIGHTS IN PRESENCE OF POLICE MAY BE HAZARDOUS TO THE HEALTH OF NON-CAUCASIANS.

ALSO INCLUDES GENUINE-LOOKING **CAMOUFLAGE** JUST LIKE **REAL** SOLDIERS WEAR!

THE FORCES OF **TYRANNY** WILL NEVER SEE ME COMING **NOW!**

IT PROBABLY LOOKS LIKE THIS GUN IS JUST **FLOATING** IN MID-AIR!

EMPTY BOX CONVERTS INTO OCCU-PIABLE **GOVERNMENT BUILDING!**

I WILL NOT BUDGE UNTIL **LIBERTY** HAS BEEN **RESTORED!**

NOW **BACK OFF,** JACK-BOOTED THUGS!

VISITOR CENTER

YOU'LL HAVE **HOURS** OF FUN ISSUING "STATEMENTS" TO THE "MEDIA"!

THE FOUNDING FATHERS **INTENDED** WESTERN CATTLE RANCHERS IN THE 21st CENTURY TO HAVE FREE GRAZING RIGHTS ON PUBLIC LAND!

AND FOR **KIDS** TO GET ALL THE ICE CREAM THEY **WANT!**

INTERESTING! TELL ME **MORE!**

VISITOR CENTER

BUT DON'T FORGET TO PACK AN EXTRA LUNCH--OR YOU MIGHT HAVE TO PUT OUT AN URGENT CALL FOR **ASSISTANCE!**

MOM!! I NEED SOME **SNACKS!**

HELLLOOO?

ORDER **YOUR** PLAYSET AND START DEFENDING FREEDOM--**TODAY!** (MANUFACTURER ACCEPTS NO LIABILITY FOR ANY DEATH, INJURY, OR PUBLIC HUMILIATION THAT MAY OCCUR.)

TOM TOMORROW ©2016

THIS MODERN WORLD

by TOM TOMORROW

MODERN COMICS GROUP

INVISIBLE-HAND-OF-THE FREE-MARKET MAN

AS A FORMER BUSINESSMAN AND VENTURE CAPITALIST, I OBVIOUSLY VALUE YOUR COUNSEL--

--BUT IF YOU'RE SUPPOSED TO BE INVISIBLE-- WHY CAN I *SEE* YOU?

SIGH... ET *TU*, GOVERNOR SNYDER?

THIS ISSUE: *CRISIS MANAGEMENT!*

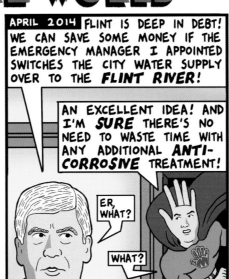

APRIL 2014 FLINT IS DEEP IN DEBT! WE CAN SAVE SOME MONEY IF THE EMERGENCY MANAGER I APPOINTED SWITCHES THE CITY WATER SUPPLY OVER TO THE *FLINT RIVER!*

AN EXCELLENT IDEA! AND I'M *SURE* THERE'S NO NEED TO WASTE TIME WITH ANY ADDITIONAL *ANTI-CORROSIVE* TREATMENT!

ER, WHAT?

WHAT?

JUNE 2014 FLINT RESIDENTS ARE COMPLAINING THAT THEIR WATER CAUSES *RASHES* AND *HAIR LOSS!*

LOOK, WE'VE *ALL* GOT TO MAKE A FEW SACRIFICES FOR AUSTERITY! TELL THEM TO BOIL THE WATER AND *STOP WHINING!*

RIGHT! UM, REMIND ME, WHAT SACRIFICES ARE *WE* MAKING?

WE HAVE TO *LISTEN* TO THEIR WHINING!

MARCH 2015 HAND, AM I EVER GLAD TO SEE *YOU!* PEOPLE ARE *STILL* COMPLAINING ABOUT THE WATER IN FLINT!

THIS IS GETTING *REALLY* TEDIOUS! LOOK, FORM AN ADVISORY COMMITTEE, PROMISE SOME IMPROVEMENTS--AND DECLARE THE PROBLEM *SOLVED!*

SEPT. 2015 A GROUP OF LOCAL PHYSICIANS CLAIM THEY'VE FOUND ELEVATED LEVELS OF LEAD IN FLINT *CHILDREN!*

ARRGH! OKAY, DENY EVERYTHING AND ACCUSE THEM OF CHERRY-PICKING THE DATA! YOU *COULD* EVEN DRINK A GLASS OF FLINT WATER YOURSELF, TO SHOW HOW *SAFE* IT IS!

UH, YEAH. MAYBE NOT.

PRESENT DAY OKAY, FINE, WE'VE BEEN POISONING FLINT WITH LEAD FOR TWO YEARS--BUT I SAID I WAS *SORRY!*

NO POINT IN PLAYING THE BLAME GAME *NOW!* TIME TO ASK FOR A HUGE FEDERAL BAILOUT--AND MOVE *ON!*

THAT'S WHAT *I* CALL RUNNING GOVERNMENT LIKE A BUSINESS!

NOW YOU MUST *EXCUSE* ME-- THERE'S A GAS LEAK IN *CALIFORNIA* THAT NEEDS MY ATTENTION!

TOM TOMORROW © 2016

THIS MODERN WORLD

by TOM TOMORROW

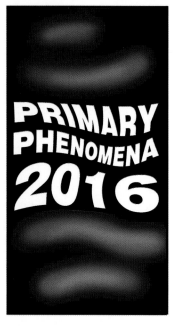

PRIMARY PHENOMENA 2016

1. THE BOTTOMLESS PIT OF INTERNECINE DISPUTE.

YOUR CANDIDATE IS FULL OF EMPTY RHETORIC!

MY CANDIDATE WILL BRING **REAL** CHANGE!

WHY MUST **YOU** BE SO **UNREALISTIC**?!

2. THE UNBEARABLE SERIOUSNESS OF VERY SERIOUS PEOPLE.

A SINGLE PAYER HEALTH CARE SYSTEM WOULD FACE **MANY** POLITICAL OBSTACLES--

--THEREFORE WE MUST NEVER SPEAK OF THE MATTER AGAIN.

SUNDAY TALKING ABOUT STUFF SHOW

3. THE MYSTERIOUS DISAPPEARING DEMOCRATIC DEBATES.

THE D.N.C. IS **EAGER** TO PROVIDE A SHOWCASE FOR BERNIE SANDERS, AND THAT OTHER GUY!

WE SCHEDULED FEWER DEBATES AT PECULIAR TIMES...IN ORDER TO, UH, **MAXIMIZE** VIEWERSHIP!

YEAH, THAT'S THE TICKET.

4. AN UNEXPECTED MAN OF PIETY.

EVANGELICALS **LOVE** ME! AND I LOVE THAT BOOK OF THEIRS, THE **BIBLE!** JESUS WAS A **GREAT** SAVIOR, ONE OF THE ALL TIME **BEST!**

5. FEAR AND LOATHING ON THE CAMPAIGN TRAIL.

AMERICA IS A **HELLHOLE**-- ON THE BRINK OF BECOMING AN EVEN **WORSE** HELL- HOLE! AND DON'T GET ME **STARTED** ON THOSE "**NEW YORK VALUES!**"

IF YOU KNOW WHAT I MEAN.

6. A POLITICAL PARTY'S DESCENT INTO MADNESS.

YARGLE BARGLE COMMUNITY ORGANIZER HOPEY CHANGEY DRILL BABY DRILL YOU BETCHA **BLARGH!**

U.S.A! U.S.A! U.S.A!

7. LIGHT AT THE END OF THE TUNNEL.

THERE ARE ONLY **TEN MORE MONTHS** 'TIL ELECTION DAY!

42 **WEEKS,** TO BE PRECISE!

BUT WHO'S COUNTING?

UM, YOU DON'T THINK TRUMP COULD REALLY **WIN,** DO YOU?

NOT UNLESS VOTERS ARE UNINFORMED, RESENTFUL, AND AFRAID!

UH OH.

TOM TOMORROW ©2016

THIS MODERN WORLD

by TOM TOMORROW

Panel 1: WELCOME BACK TO THE *ELECTION NEWS NETWORK*! OUR TOP STORY: NUMEROUS PEOPLE ARE RUNNING FOR PRESIDENT--BUT ONLY *ONE* OF THEM IS GOING TO *WIN*!

BUT WHICH *ONE*? WHICH ONE WILL IT *BE*?

HUH?

HUH?

Panel 2: JOINING US TO DISCUSS THE UN-EXPECTEDLY CLOSE RACE BETWEEN BERNIE SANDERS AND HILLARY CLINTON IS OUR FREQUENT GUEST, THE *DEMOCRATIC STRATEGIST*!

LOOK, PEOPLE SHOULD NOT VOTE FOR BERNIE SANDERS, BECAUSE HE CANNOT WIN.

UNLESS PEOPLE VOTE FOR HIM. WHICH THEY SHOULD NOT.

Panel 3: SANDERS IS A *SOCIALIST* WHO WANTS TO IMPOSE *SOCIALIZED MEDICINE* AND USED TO HANG OUT WITH HIS SOCIALIST BUDDIES IN THE *SOVIET UNION*--

--ARE ALL THINGS *REPUBLICANS* WILL SAY IF HE'S THE NOMINEE! THEY'LL TEAR HIM *APART*!

UNLIKE HILLARY CLINTON, WHO THEY WILL TREAT WITH KID GLOVES AND THE GREATEST RESPECT.

I SEE!

Panel 4: ON THE *REPUBLICAN* SIDE, THE SURPRISE FRONT RUNNER HAS, OF COURSE, BEEN *DONALD TRUMP*! HERE TO EXAMINE *HIS* APPEAL TO RANK-AND-FILE VOTERS IS OUR REGULAR COMMENTATOR, THE *REASONABLE REPUBLICAN*!

IT'S A REAL PUZZLE, BIFF!

Panel 5: HE'S RACIST, MISOGYNISTIC AND AUTHORITARIAN! HE *ENCOURAGES* RESENTMENT AND HOSTILITY!

WHAT *POSSIBLE* PRECEDENT HAS THERE BEEN FOR SUCH A PHENO-MENON IN REPUBLICAN POLITICS?

ER-- WELL--

NONE, I TELL YOU! *NO PRECEDENT*!

IT'S JUST A MYSTERY BEYOND HUMAN COMPREHENSION.

Panel 6: OKAY THEN! COMING UP NEXT-- WE'LL TAKE AN EVEN *CLOSER* LOOK AT THESE OUTSIDER CANDIDATES!

ONE IS A LEGISLATOR WITH DECADES OF EXPERIENCE--THE OTHER IS A REALITY TV STAR WHO SPENDS A LOT OF TIME INSULTING PEOPLE ON *TWITTER*--

--IN OTHER WORDS, *TWO SIDES* OF THE *SAME COIN*!

HA HA! YOU GOT *THAT* RIGHT, WANDA!

FIRST THESE MES-SAGES.

TOM TOMORROW©2016

THIS MODERN WORLD

by TOM TOMORROW

PRIMARY QUESTIONS

AN ONGOING SERIES

THAT GOES ON AND ON AND ON

1. WHAT DEFINES A "REAL" PROGRESSIVE?

IT'S A *FASCINATING* QUESTION-- WHICH I WAS JUST DISCUSSING WITH MY GOOD FRIEND, DOCTOR *HENRY KISSINGER!*

?

2. *CAN* A 74-YEAR-OLD SOCIALIST FROM VERMONT WIN THE GENERAL ELECTION?

COMING UP NEXT--WILL BERNIE SANDERS REDISTRIBUTE *YOUR* WEALTH?

AND PUT YOU IN A RE-EDUCATION CAMP?

OUR EXPERTS WEIGH IN!

Action McNews Network

3. WHAT KIND OF POLITICAL NAIF WOULD THINK THAT LARGE SPEECH FEES FROM INVESTMENT BANKS ARE SOMEHOW *PROBLEMATIC*?

IT WAS JUST STANDARD PAYMENT-- FOR SPEECHES THAT *HAPPENED* TO BE GIVEN BY A PROBABLE FUTURE *PRESIDENT!*

THEY COULD JUST AS EASILY HAVE GRABBED SOME HOBO OFF THE *STREET!*

4. SHOULD CANDIDATES BE JUDGED BY THE WORST OF THEIR FOLLOWERS?

THE "BERNIE BROS" ON TWITTER ARE *UNSPEAKABLY* VILE!

AND THE INTERNET IS USUALLY SUCH A *CIVIL* PLACE!

IT CERTAINLY REFLECTS POORLY ON HIS CRITIQUE OF INCOME INEQUALITY!

5. IS IT POSSIBLE TO GO INTO CRYOGENIC SUSPENSION UNTIL 2017? OR AT LEAST UNTIL THE END OF THE PRIMARY SEASON?

ASKING FOR A FRIEND.

yargle

bargle

blargh

TOM TOMORROW ©2016

110

THIS MODERN WORLD

by TOM TOMORROW

SUNDAY TALKING ABOUT STUFF SHOW

WELCOME, EVERYONE! OUR TOPIC THIS MORNING IS, OF COURSE, THE UNTIMELY PASSING OF JUSTICE ANTONIN SCALIA!

JOINING ME TO DISCUSS THE RAMIFICATIONS OF HIS DEATH ARE MY GOOD FRIENDS, THE *GENERIC CONSERVATIVE PUNDITS!*

OBVIOUSLY THE DEATH OF A VIRULENT IDEOLOGUE AT THE CENTER OF COUNTLESS BITTER POLITICAL DEBATES SHOULD NEVER BE *POLITICIZED!*

AND OF COURSE, *ANY* APPOINTMENT BY OBAMA WOULD BE *INHERENTLY* POLITICAL!

I *SEE!*

A LAME-DUCK PRESIDENT WITH A MERE *YEAR* REMAINING IN HIS FINAL TERM SHOULD *NOT* GET TO PICK A SUPREME COURT JUSTICE!

HE SHOULD WAIT UNTIL THE *NEXT* PRESIDENT IS ELECTED!

ASSUMING *THAT* PRESIDENT IS A REPUBLICAN.

OTHERWISE, THE ONE AFTER *THAT!*

IT'S WHAT THE FOUNDING FATHERS INTENDED, EVEN IF THEY DID NOT SPECIFICALLY MENTION IT IN THE CONSTITUTION!

IT'S PRETTY MUCH *IMPLIED!*

AS JUSTICE SCALIA WOULD NO DOUBT HAVE *AGREED!*

WELL, HE *WAS* AN ORIGINALIST!

NEXT: A LOOK BACK AT AN EXTRAORDINARY LEGAL MIND!

REMEMBER THAT TIME HE RULED THAT SOMEONE CAN BE EXECUTED EVEN IF NEW EVIDENCE PROVES THEIR *INNOCENCE?*

OR THAT TIME HE CALLED THE VOTING RIGHTS ACT A "PERPETUATION OF RACIAL *ENTITLEMENT*"?

TALK ABOUT *MEMORIES!*

TOM TOMORROW ©2016

THIS MODERN WORLD

by TOM TOMORROW

LISTEN: SPARKY THE PENGUIN HAS COME UNSTUCK IN TIME...

UH--HELLO! WHAT YEAR IS THIS?

2014. AND WHAT YEAR MIGHT **YOU** BE FROM?

EARLY 2016.

POP!

INTERESTING! SO--ARE YOU ALREADY BORED TO TEARS BY THE INEVITABLE MATCHUP BETWEEN **HILLARY CLINTON** AND **JEB BUSH**?

UM, WELL--THAT'S NOT **EXACTLY** HOW THINGS TURNED OUT.

HILLARY HAS BEEN FACING AN UNEXPECTEDLY STRONG CHALLENGE-- FROM A CRANKY, 74-YEAR-OLD SELF-AVOWED **SOCIALIST**!

HUH. WELL, **THAT'S** KIND OF AWESOME.

I QUITE CONCUR!

I THOUGHT YOU MIGHT.

MEANWHILE, **JEB** HAS DROPPED OUT OF THE RACE--AND AT THIS POINT, IT'S ENTIRELY POSSIBLE THE **REPUBLICAN** NOMINEE WILL BE--

--SCOTT WALKER? CARLY FIORINA? **CHRIS CHRISTIE**?

--DONALD **TRUMP**.

THEN AGAIN, MAYBE YOU'RE FROM A DYSTOPIAN **ALTERNATE** TIMELINE.

YOU CAN ONLY HOPE.

NEXT TIME GUYS! **I'M** FROM 2024-- AND YOU WOULD NOT **BELIEVE** WHAT EMPEROR TRUMP HAS DECREED **NOW**!

POP!

TOM TOMORROW © 2016

112

THIS MODERN WORLD

by TOM TOMORROW

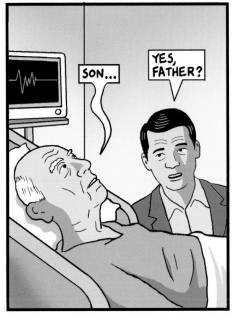

SON...

YES, FATHER?

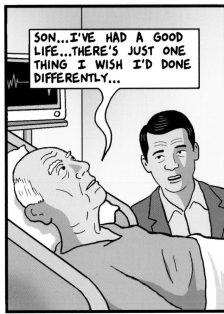

SON...I'VE HAD A GOOD LIFE...THERE'S JUST ONE THING I WISH I'D DONE DIFFERENTLY...

I WISH...

I WISH...

WHAT IS IT, FATHER?

I WISH I'D SPENT MORE TIME ARGUING WITH RANDOS ON TWITTER.

BEEEEEEEEEEEEEEEEEP

LIFE'S TOO SHORT FOR REGRETS.

hey moron your opinion sucks lol

TAP TAP TAP

Tom Tomorrow ©2016

THIS MODERN WORLD

by TOM TOMORROW

TRUMP MANIA
CRAZY IS THE NEW NORMAL

VETTING THE CANDIDATE

HE'S A *CELEBRITY* WHO WILL MAKE AMERICA *GREAT* AGAIN!

WHAT FURTHER QUALIFICATION COULD HE POSSIBLY *NEED*?

A SURPRISE ENDORSEMENT

DONALD TRUMP IS THE KINDEST, WARMEST, BRAVEST, MOST WONDERFUL HUMAN BEING I'VE EVER KNOWN.

I TOTALLY BELIEVE THESE THINGS I AM SAYING.

ELEVATED DISCOURSE

DONALD HAS TINY HANDS! BY WHICH I MEAN A *SMALL PENIS*!

WHAT IF HE'S IN A LOCKER ROOM WITH *PUTIN* SOMEDAY?

LIAR! IT'S *YUUUUGE*!

THE ELEPHANT IN THE ROOM

"RACISM"? I'VE NEVER EVEN *HEARD* THIS WORD BEFORE!

I'LL NEED SOME TIME TO *RESEARCH* THE MATTER BEFORE I CAN COMMENT!

DENIAL'S NOT A RIVER

TRUMP'S POPULARITY IS *DEFINITELY* NOT THE RESULT OF DECADES OF REPUBLICAN DOG-WHISTLE POLITICS!

I BLAME *OBAMA*, FOR REASONS I WILL EXPLAIN AS SOON AS I THINK OF THEM.

SERIOUSLY, NOT A RIVER

DEMOCRATS WILL BEAT HIM *EASILY*-- ONCE WE POINT OUT TO VOTERS THAT HE IS A BOORISH, RACE-BAITING *NARCISSIST*!

THEY MIGHT NOT HAVE *NOTICED*!

MEN OF GREAT PRINCIPLE

DONALD TRUMP IS A DANGEROUS LUNATIC WHO MUST BE *STOPPED*!

UNLESS HE WINS THE NOMINATION, IN WHICH CASE WE PLEDGE TO SUPPORT HIM.

THE UNKNOWABLE FUTURE

WOW, NO ONE COULD HAVE FORESEEN HOW *THIS* ELECTION WOULD TURN OUT! AND NOW IT'S IN THE HANDS OF THE *SUPREME COURT*!

THE *EIGHT-MEMBER* SUPREME COURT!

THAT'S THE ONE!

ion News work   Action McNews Network   Ac Mc Net

TOM TOMORROW ©2016

114

THIS MODERN WORLD

by TOM TOMORROW

FURTHER PRIMARY PHENOMENA

MORE NOTES FROM THE LONG SLOG TO ELECTION DAY

WHICH IS STILL VERY FAR AWAY

REFLEXIVE EVASION

I'D BE *HAPPY* TO RELEASE THE TRANSCRIPTS OF MY WALL STREET SPEECHES--

--JUST AS SOON AS EVERY HUMAN BEING ON THE PLANET RELEASES TRANSCRIPTS OF ANY SPEECHES *THEY* MAY HAVE GIVEN!

I MEAN, FAIR'S *FAIR!*

THE AUDACITY OF PRAGMATISM

FREE TUITION AND SINGLE PAYER HEALTH CARE ARE NAIVE, IDEALISTIC *FANTASIES!*

YOU KNOW WHAT *REALLY* MOTIVATES VOTERS? *CAUTIOUS INCRE-MENTALISM!*

CONFIRMATION BIAS

DID YOU *SEE* THE WAY SANDERS WAGGED HIS FINGER AND LOOKED VAGUELY ANNOYED DURING THE LAST DEBATE?

I CERTAINLY *DID!* IS THERE NO *END* TO HIS CONTEMPTUOUS MISOGYNY?

MANIFEST DESTINY

IT'S TIME FOR SANDERS TO DROP OUT--AND BACK THE *REAL* NOMINEE!

WHY, HIS CAM-PAIGN WOULD BE OVER AL-READY--

--IF PEOPLE WOULD JUST STOP *VOTING* FOR HIM!

MEANWHILE AT THE GATES OF HELL

I'M A *UNIFIER!* THE *GREATEST!* PEOPLE *LOVE* ME--OR ELSE THEY SHOULD BE PUNCHED IN THE *FACE!*

ALL HAIL *TRUMP!!*

TOM TOMORROW ©2016

THIS MODERN WORLD

by TOM TOMORROW

2016 · AMAZING SUPER-CLASSY COMICS

THE INCREDIBLE TRUMP

TRUMP **SMASH**-- --THE REPUBLICAN **PARTY!**

A HARDWORKING BUSINESSMAN EXAMINES AN EXPERIMENTAL PROTOTYPE...

MY INVENTION CONVERTS HUMAN EMOTIONS--SPECIFICALLY, THE ANGER AND RESENTMENT OF THE WHITE WORKING CLASS--

--INTO A VIABLE SOURCE OF ENERGY WHICH CAN POWER ENTIRE **BUILDINGS!**

HEY, I COULD USE **THAT** IN MY MANY CLASSY SKYSCRAPERS AND RESORTS!

BUT SOMETHING GOES TERRIBLY **WRONG!**

TRUMP FEEL POWER **SURGING** THROUGH BODY--BUT TRUMP WANT **MORE!**

TRUMP WANT **PRESIDENCY!**

SOON...

TRUMP THINK MEXICANS ARE RAPISTS AND DRUG SMUGGLERS, AND **SOME**, TRUMP ASSUME, ARE GOOD PEOPLE.

WOMAN WITH BLOOD COMING OUT OF HER WHEREVER MAKE TRUMP **ANGRY!** YOU WON'T **LIKE** TRUMP WHEN HE'S **ANGRY!**

TRUMP WANT TO PUNCH PROTESTERS IN **FACE**--LIKE IN GOOD OLD DAYS WHEN AMERICA WAS **GREAT!**

THE PARTY ESTABLISHMENT **TRIES** TO TAKE HIM DOWN.

YOU CAN'T VOTE FOR HIM! HE'S **OPENLY** RACIST AND XENOPHOBIC!

REAL REPUBLICANS USE CODED **DOG WHISTLES!**

HA HA! YOUR PUNY ATTACKS CANNOT STOP **TRUMP!**

BUT--CAN HE TRIUMPH IN THE **GENERAL ELECTION?**

HE MAY BE AN UNTHINKING, RAGEFILLED **MONSTER**--

--BUT AT LEAST HE'S NOT A **CAREER POLITICIAN!**

NEXT: A LOYAL **SIDEKICK!**

YOU! SCRAPE TRUMP'S **TOENAIL FUNGUS!**

YES **SIR!**

TOM TOMORROW ©2016

116

THIS MODERN WORLD

by TOM TOMORROW

Panel 1:
IT'S YOU AGAIN! BACK TO CONDUCT FURTHER ANTHROPOLOGICAL RESEARCH?

AFFIRMATIVE! I HAVE BEEN MONITORING YOUR PLANETARY COMMUNICATION NETWORKS FROM AFAR--

Panel 2:
--BUT NOW IT IS TIME ONCE AGAIN TO OBSERVE FIRSTHAND THE INEXPLICABLY LONG AND TEDIOUS PROCESS BY WHICH YOUR NATION-STATE SELECTS A NEW *LEADER!*

Panel 3:
THE INTERNAL DIVISIONS OF THE IDEOLOGICAL-SLASH-TRIBAL GROUPING KNOWN AS "DEMOCRATS" HAVE INTRODUCED SOME INTRIGUING UNCERTAINTY INTO WHAT PREVIOUSLY APPEARED TO BE A PRE-DETERMINED OUTCOME--

Panel 4:
--BUT IT IS THE "REPUBLICANS" WHO ARE *TRULY* FASCINATING! THEIR VOTERS APPEAR TO VIEW IGNORANCE, PARANOIA, AND REFLEXIVE HOSTILITY AS *QUALIFICATIONS* FOR LEADERSHIP!

Panel 5:
HOW COULD I *NOT* RETURN? IT IS AN *EXTRAORDINARY* OPPORTUNITY TO OBSERVE A SOCIETY TEETERING ON THE BRINK OF SELF-IMMOLATION!

ER, YES, WELL--

Panel 6:
--PERHAPS YOU COULD HELP US OUT SOMEHOW? WITH YOUR ADVANCED KNOWLEDGE AND TECHNOLOGY?

I'M SORRY--I AM ONLY ALLOWED TO OBSERVE, NOT TO INTERFERE.

Panel 7:

Panel 8:
UNLESS *TRUMP* WINS, OF COURSE. THEN I'LL HAVE TO VAPORIZE YOUR PLANET, JUST TO BE SAFE.

NOTHING PERSONAL.

I UNDERSTAND COMPLETELY.

TOM TOMORROW © 2016

THIS MODERN WORLD

by TOM TOMORROW

AS WE HAVE PREVIOUSLY SEEN... A TWIST OF FATE TURNS AN ORDINARY EGOMANIACAL BILLIONAIRE INTO...

THE INCREDIBLE TRUMP

TRUMP *SMASH*--

--ALL STANDARDS OF PROPRIETY!

HANDS NOT SO SMALL *NOW*, LOSERS AND HATERS!

HE REALIZES THAT HE, ALONE, HAS THE STRENGTH TO PROPERLY LEAD AMERICA!

TRUMP WILL SMASH SO MANY ENEMIES--YOU'LL GET *TIRED* OF ENEMY-SMASHING! BELIEVE TRUMP-- IT WILL BE *TREMENDOUS!*

HE MAY BE AN ORANGE RAGE-MONSTER--BUT HE KNOWS WHAT THE *REAL* PROBLEM IS!

ALL THIS *POLITICAL CORRECTNESS* MAKE TRUMP *SICK!* WE CAN'T TORTURE TERRORISTS--*OR* SAY "MERRY CHRISTMAS"!

WHEN *TRUMP* IS PRESIDENT, WE WILL TORTURE TERRORISTS *AND* SAY "MERRY CHRISTMAS"--

--MAYBE AT SAME *TIME!*

FIRST, HE MUST BATTLE HIS PUNY *RIVALS*...

TRUMP'S WIFE *MUCH* HOTTER THAN *YOURS*, LYIN' TED!

NOW YOU LISTEN HERE, DONALD, THIS BEHAVIOR IS SIMPLY *UN-ACCEPTABLE!*

HA! HA! HA! YOU THINK NORMAL RULES APPLY TO *TRUMP?* SAD!

NOT TO MENTION THE *MEDIA*...

STUPID LADY REPORTER SAY TRUMP CAMPAIGN MANAGER *GRAB* HER-- BUT MAYBE SHE WAS TRYING TO HURT *TRUMP!*

PEN IN HER HAND *MIGHT* HAVE BEEN *LITTLE BOMB!*

TRUMP FEAR *NOTHING*, BUT HEY, YOU CAN'T BE TOO CAREFUL.

MEANWHILE, THE CLARITY OF HIS MESSAGE CONTINUES TO *RESONATE!*

TRUMP *CHERISH* WOMEN--ESPECIALLY *HOT* ONES! ALSO, YOU SHOULD *SEE* MARBLE FINISHES IN TRUMP'S NEW *HOTEL*, WHICH WENT UP AHEAD OF SCHEDULE AND IS VERY HIGH QUALITY--THE *BEST!*

HE SURE SAYS WHAT HE *THINKS!*

THERE'S NO ONE *I'D* RATHER HAVE IN CHARGE OF THE NUCLEAR CODES!

TOM TOMORROW © 2016

THIS MODERN WORLD

by TOM TOMORROW

THESE YOUNG PEOPLE SUPPORTING BERNIE SANDERS ARE SO **NAIVE!** WHY CAN'T THEY GROW UP--AND GET BEHIND THE **SENSIBLE** CANDIDATE?

OH BOY--HERE WE GO.

THERE'S ABSOLUTELY NO **WAY** SANDERS COULD EVER WIN THE GENERAL ELECTION!

YOU SAY THAT WITH SUCH **CONFIDENCE!** DO YOU HAVE PREVIOUSLY-UNDISCLOSED POWERS OF **PRECOGNITION?**

LOOK--IF WE END UP WITH PRESIDENT **TRUMP** OR **CRUZ,** WE'LL HAVE **BERNIE SANDERS'** LEFT-WING FOLLOWERS TO **THANK.**

YOU KNOW, IT'S NOT AS IF THEY'RE MOUNTING A THIRD PARTY **INSURGENCY** HERE--

PERISH THE **THOUGHT!**

--BUT IF YOU THINK IT'S SOMEHOW **ILLEGITIMATE** OF THEM TO SUPPORT THE CANDIDATE THEY PREFER--**IN THE DEMOCRATIC PRIMARY**--

IT **HAS** BEEN AN UNNECESSARY COMPLICATION!

--**WHEN,** EXACTLY, WOULD YOU CONSIDER THEIR PARTICIPATION IN THIS PROCESS **ACCEPTABLE?**

ER--WELL--

--MAYBE THEY COULD GO MARCH WITH SOME GIANT **PUPPETS** SOMEWHERE! DON'T LEFTIES ENJOY THAT SORT OF THING?

THIS IS GOING TO BE A LONG COUPLE OF MONTHS, ISN'T IT?

SEEMS LIKELY.

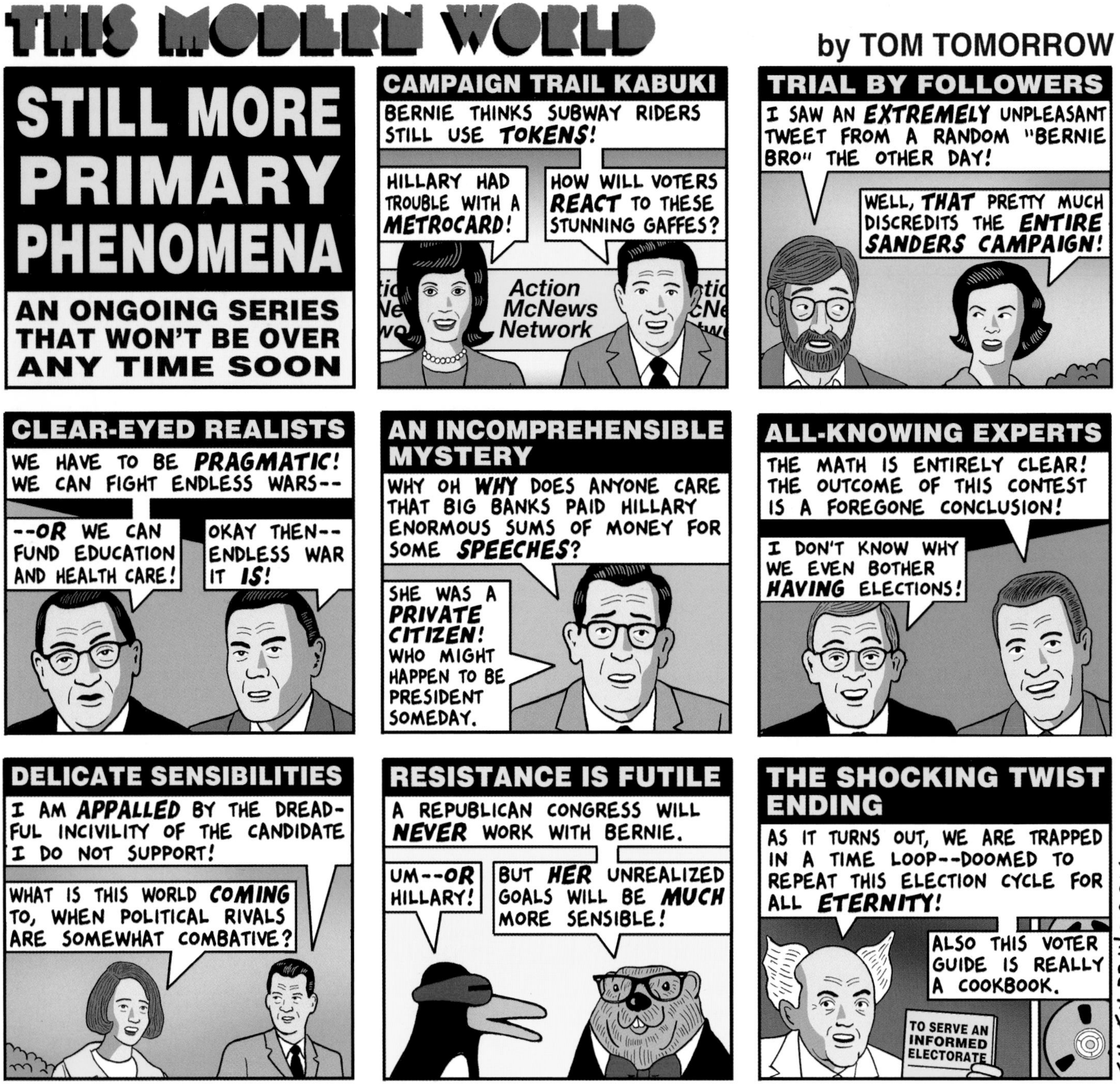
THIS MODERN WORLD
by TOM TOMORROW
STILL MORE PRIMARY PHENOMENA
AN ONGOING SERIES THAT WON'T BE OVER ANY TIME SOON
CAMPAIGN TRAIL KABUKI
BERNIE THINKS SUBWAY RIDERS STILL USE TOKENS!
HILLARY HAD TROUBLE WITH A METROCARD!
HOW WILL VOTERS REACT TO THESE STUNNING GAFFES?
Action McNews Network
TRIAL BY FOLLOWERS
I SAW AN EXTREMELY UNPLEASANT TWEET FROM A RANDOM "BERNIE BRO" THE OTHER DAY!
WELL, THAT PRETTY MUCH DISCREDITS THE ENTIRE SANDERS CAMPAIGN!
CLEAR-EYED REALISTS
WE HAVE TO BE PRAGMATIC! WE CAN FIGHT ENDLESS WARS--
--OR WE CAN FUND EDUCATION AND HEALTH CARE!
OKAY THEN--ENDLESS WAR IT IS!
AN INCOMPREHENSIBLE MYSTERY
WHY OH WHY DOES ANYONE CARE THAT BIG BANKS PAID HILLARY ENORMOUS SUMS OF MONEY FOR SOME SPEECHES?
SHE WAS A PRIVATE CITIZEN! WHO MIGHT HAPPEN TO BE PRESIDENT SOMEDAY.
ALL-KNOWING EXPERTS
THE MATH IS ENTIRELY CLEAR! THE OUTCOME OF THIS CONTEST IS A FOREGONE CONCLUSION!
I DON'T KNOW WHY WE EVEN BOTHER HAVING ELECTIONS!
DELICATE SENSIBILITIES
I AM APPALLED BY THE DREADFUL INCIVILITY OF THE CANDIDATE I DO NOT SUPPORT!
WHAT IS THIS WORLD COMING TO, WHEN POLITICAL RIVALS ARE SOMEWHAT COMBATIVE?
RESISTANCE IS FUTILE
A REPUBLICAN CONGRESS WILL NEVER WORK WITH BERNIE.
UM--OR HILLARY!
BUT HER UNREALIZED GOALS WILL BE MUCH MORE SENSIBLE!
THE SHOCKING TWIST ENDING
AS IT TURNS OUT, WE ARE TRAPPED IN A TIME LOOP--DOOMED TO REPEAT THIS ELECTION CYCLE FOR ALL ETERNITY!
ALSO THIS VOTER GUIDE IS REALLY A COOKBOOK.
TO SERVE AN INFORMED ELECTORATE
TOM TOMORROW© 2016

THIS MODERN WORLD

by TOM TOMORROW

THE INCREDIBLE TRUMP

THIS WEEK: VICTORY WITHIN *GRASP!*

TRUMP SMASH *ANY* PUNY CARTOONIST WHO DRAW WHITE HOUSE WITH GIANT "TRUMP" SIGN ON TOP!

TRUMP THINK *THAT* JOKE ALREADY DONE TO *DEATH!*

SO FAR, HE'S BEEN CAMPAIGNING AS AN UNRESTRAINED ORANGE RAGE MONSTER--WITH GREAT *SUCCESS*--

LYIN' *TED!* MEXICAN *RAPISTS!* POLITICAL *CORRECTNESS!* THE TERRIBLE, TERRIBLE *MEDIA!*

TRUMP SMASH *EVERYTHING!*

--BUT NOW IT'S TIME TO ACT *PRESIDENTIAL.*

TRUMP CAN DO THAT! TRUMP WILL BE MORE PRESIDENTIAL THAN *ANYONE,* INCLUDING FORMER PRESIDENTS!

WHOOPS, TRUMP ACCIDENTALLY RETWEET ANOTHER WHITE SUPREMACIST.

CAN HE SUPPRESS THE VERY FORCE WHICH SUSTAINS HIM AND GIVES HIM *POWER?*

TRUMP--ER--VERY PLEASED TO--UH--SPEAK IN POLITE AND MEASURED TONES ABOUT DISTINGUISHED RIVAL--

--SENATOR LYIN' TED!

AND DOES HE EVEN WANT TO?

AAARGH! TRUMP CAN'T *STAND* IT! TRUMP *SMASH* GULLIBLE MEDIA CONSENSUS ABOUT TRUMP'S PRESIDENTIAL *DEMEANOR!*

TRUMP *HOPE* CONVENTION NOT VIOLENT--

--BUT TRUMP NOT MAKING ANY *PROMISES!*

MEANWHILE, THEY'RE FEELING OPTIMISTIC OVER AT THE D.N.C.

ACCORDING TO THE NBC NEWS/WALL STREET JOURNAL POLL, 68% OF VOTERS COULD *NEVER* IMAGINE VOTING FOR TRUMP--

--BUT ONLY 58% FEEL THAT WAY ABOUT *HILLARY!*

WE'LL *DEMOLISH* HIM--WITH OUR *TEN-PERCENT-LESS-DESPISED* ADVANTAGE!

TOM TOMORROW ©2016

121

THIS MODERN WORLD

by TOM TOMORROW

THE FOREVER CAMPAIGN

AN EXPLOSION IN THE FABRIC OF TIME SCATTERS THE 2016 PRESIDENTIAL RACE THROUGHOUT HISTORY.

SORRY!

MY BAD!

BACK IN THE MESOZOIC ERA, PUNDITS EXPECT A SNOOZEFEST.

OBVIOUSLY IT'S GOING TO BE A TEDIOUS MATCHUP BETWEEN **JEB** AND **HILLARY!**

THE ONLY QUESTION IS--WILL SHE STOMP HIM LIKE A **T-REX--** OR BE DEVOURED LIKE A HAPLESS **HADROSAUR?**

ONLY **TIME** WILL TELL! HA HA!

AT THE HEIGHT OF THE ROMAN EMPIRE, SEVENTEEN REPUBLICAN HOPEFULS COMPETE FOR THE ATTENTION OF VOTERS.

I COME TO **BURY** OBAMACARE, NOT TO PRAISE IT!

I CAME, I SAW, AND--UH-- I FORGET THE THIRD ONE.

THE FIELD BEGINS TO THIN OUT DURING THE AMERICAN REVOLUTION.

I REGRET THAT I HAVE BUT ONE CAMPAIGN TO GIVE FOR MY COUNTRY!

GIVE **ME** VICTORY-- OR GIVE ME **CRUSHING INDIFFERENCE!**

SOMEDAY IN THE DISTANT FUTURE, IT WILL ALL BE OVER.

IN THE RACE BETWEEN HILLARY CLINTON'S UPLOADED CONSCIOUSNESS AND DONALD TRUMP'S CRYOGENICALLY PRESERVED BRAIN, THE WINNER IS--

--OH, NEVERMIND. I'VE JUST BEEN INFORMED THE HEAT DEATH OF THE UNIVERSE IS **IMMINENT.**

BUT FIRST-- THESE MESSAGES!

AKSHUN MCNEWZ NETWERK

MEANWHILE IN **CANADA** IN THE YEAR 2016...

CAN YOU **BELIEVE** LAST YEAR'S ELECTION DRAGGED ON FOR **ELEVEN FULL WEEKS**, START TO FINISH?

IT FELT LIKE AN **ETERNITY**, EH?

TOM TOMORROW ©2016

THIS MODERN WORLD

by TOM TOMORROW

2016 AMAZING SUPER-CLASSY COMICS

THE INCREDIBLE TRUMP

HOW--HOW COULD G.O.P. VOTERS CHOOSE A LUNATIC WHO PANDERS TO THEIR WORST INSTINCTS--

--WHO ISN'T ME?

PRIMARY PANDEMONIUM!

WITH HIS VICTORY IN INDIANA, THE INCREDIBLE TRUMP BECOMES THE PRESUMPTIVE G.O.P. NOMINEE.

HA HA! TRUMP SMASH PATHETIC LYIN' TED--

--BUT TRUMP SO PRESIDENTIAL, TRUMP ALSO PRAISE LYIN' TED AS TOUGH, SMART GUY--

--WHOSE FATHER MAY OR MAY NOT HAVE BEEN INVOLVED IN THE KENNEDY ASSASSINATION!

TRUMP READ ABOUT IT IN NATIONAL ENQUIRER.

PUNDITS STRUGGLE TO EXPLAIN HIS PHENOMENAL RISE.

HE CLEARLY DERIVES HIS IMMENSE POWER FROM THE ANGER AND RESENTMENT OF WHITE CONSERVATIVES!

BUT ISN'T THEIR ANGER A DIRECT RESPONSE TO LIBERAL SMUGNESS?

AREN'T TV COMEDIANS ULTIMATELY TO BLAME?

SOUNDS LIKE A HOT TAKE TO ME!

SUNDAY TALKING ABOUT STUFF SHOW

MAYBE IT'S BECAUSE HE'S NOT AFRAID TO SAY WHAT HE THINKS!

GLOBAL WARMING IS A HOAX! SCALIA WAS MURDERED! MUSLIMS IN NEW JERSEY CELEBRATED ON 9/11!

PUNY FACT CHECKERS COMPLAIN-- BUT TRUMP ONLY KNOW WHAT TRUMP READ ON INTERNET!

AND IN NATIONAL ENQUIRER.

IN ANY CASE, THE DATA JOURNALISTS NEVER SAW IT COMING.

YES, MISTAKES WERE MADE--BUT PLEASE DON'T LET THIS DAMAGE YOUR OPINION OF OUR BRAND!

DATA JOURNALISM CAN NEVER FAIL-- IT CAN ONLY BE FAILED!

BAH! TRUMP SMASH PUNY DATA WONKS!

NOR, FOR THAT MATTER, DID THE REPUBLICAN PARTY.

I GUESS HE'S NOT SO BAD--AS IGNORANT RAGE MONSTERS GO!

THE INCREDIBLE TRUMP IS THE KINDEST, WARMEST, BRAVEST, MOST WONDERFUL BEING I'VE EVER KNOWN IN MY LIFE.

REPUBLICAN NATIONAL COMMITTEE

HELLO REINCE

NEXT TIME: THE NATIONS OF THE WORLD OFFER TO HELP BUILD A WALL--TO KEEP AMERICA IN!

ToM TOMORROW ©2016

THIS MODERN WORLD

by TOM TOMORROW

Panel 1: I BELIEVE THIS NATION SHOULD COMMIT ITSELF TO ACHIEVING THE GOAL, BEFORE THIS DECADE IS OUT, OF LANDING A MAN ON THE MOON AND RETURNING HIM SAFELY TO *EARTH!*

Panel 2: **SOON** THE PRESIDENT'S GOAL IS *AMBITIOUS*--BUT IT'S CERTAINLY NOT VERY *PRAGMATIC!*

HE SHOULD *REALLY* TONE DOWN THE *ASPIRATIONAL RHETORIC!* THERE'S NO PLACE FOR THAT SORT OF THING IN *AMERICAN* POLITICS!

Sunday Talking About Stuff Show

Panel 3: ANYWAY, WE *ALREADY* SENT A MAN INTO *ORBIT!*

DO WE WANT TO RISK UNDERMINING *THAT* ACHIEVEMENT--BY ATTEMPTING SOMETHING THAT MIGHT *NOT* SUCCEED?

Sunday Talking About Stuff Show

Panel 4: WHAT ARE THE *PRECISE DETAILS* OF THIS SO-CALLED PLAN? HOW *EXACTLY* CAN A ROCKET ACHIEVE ESCAPE VELOCITY AND REACH A TARGET 238,900 MILES AWAY?

IF WE DON'T KNOW THE ANSWER TO EVERY QUESTION IN ADVANCE--THEN WE SHOULDN'T EVEN *TRY!*

Sunday Talking About Stuff Show

Panel 5: AND LET'S NOT FORGET THE *MONEY* THAT MIGHT OTHERWISE BE SPENT ON SOMETHING *SENSIBLE*--

--LIKE *GUNS!* AND *BOMBS!*

THE AMERICAN PEOPLE ARE *FAR* TOO LEVEL-HEADED TO EMBRACE *THIS* CRAZY SCHEME!

Sunday Talking About Stuff Show

Panel 6: **AND SO** WHAT I *MEANT* TO SAY IS, WE SHOULD FORM AN *EXPLORATORY COMMITTEE* BEFORE THE DECADE IS OUT--TO CONSIDER THE POSSIBILITY OF *MAYBE* LANDING A MAN ON THE MOON *SOMEDAY!*

AS LONG AS IT'S NOT TOO DIFFICULT, AND THE PUNDITS APPROVE.

...AND HISTORY MARCHES *ONWARD!*

TOM TOMORROW ©2016

124

THIS MODERN WORLD

by TOM TOMORROW

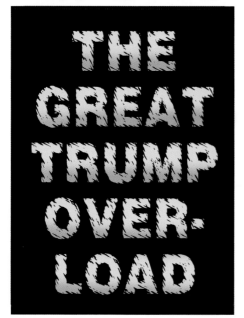

THE GREAT TRUMP OVER-LOAD

IT'S A RELENTLESS ONSLAUGHT OF ABSURDITY.

NO YOU *CAN'T* SEE MY TAX RETURNS, HATERS!

I *RESPECT* WOMEN, ESPECIALLY THE HOT ONES I CAN DRESS UP IN BIKINIS!

PEOPLE WHO COMPLAIN WHEN I RETWEET NAZIS ARE SUCH *LOSERS!*

SAD!

SATIRE AND REALITY ARE INCREASINGLY INDISTINGUISHABLE.

THIS IS MY NEW MEDIA SPOKESMAN, A TREMENDOUS INDIVIDUAL-- *SOCKY McSOCKFACE!*

THANK YOU MR. TRUMP! YOU ARE TRULY A GRACIOUS MAN WHO EVERYONE LOVES, THAT I CAN TELL YOU!

AND WHAT NORMAL HANDS YOU HAVE, IF I DO SAY SO MYSELF!

EVENTUALLY OUR BRAINS WILL JUST SHORT-CIRCUIT AND NO ONE WILL BE ABLE TO PROCESS ANY OF IT ANYMORE.

DONALD TRUMP AND HIS RACIST BUTLER JUST ROBBED A BANK WHILE SCREAMING OBSCENITIES ABOUT OBAMA'S BIRTH CERTIFICATE!

OH WELL! MORE OF THE SAME OLD SAME OLD!

IT'S JUST TRUMP BEING *TRUMP!*

WE WON'T BE ABLE TO REMEMBER WHAT IT WAS EVER LIKE BEFORE.

TRUMP SAYS IF *HE'S* ELECTED, HE WON'T RULE OUT USING *NUKES* ON STATES THAT DIDN'T VOTE FOR HIM!

ALSO, HE BIT THE HEAD OFF A LIVE BUNNY.

THIS IS JUST LIKE EVERY OTHER CAMPAIGN SEASON EVER, EXCEPT EVEN MORE NORMAL!

I THINK?

BUT AT LEAST IF HE LOSES, IT'LL ALL BE OVER IN SIX MONTHS...RIGHT?

CROOKED HILLARY DIDN'T *WIN*-- SHE *STOLE* THE ELECTION! *SAD!* MR. TRUMP IS THE *REAL* PRESIDENT-ELECT, THAT I CAN TELL YOU!

HE *HOPES* THERE'S NOT AN ARMED UPRISING OF ANGRY WHITE NATIONALISTS--

--BUT HE CAN'T MAKE ANY *PROMISES!*

Tom Tomorrow ©2016

THIS MODERN WORLD

by TOM TOMORROW

YET ANOTHER INSTALLMENT OF PRIMARY PHENOMENA

NOTES FROM THE ROAD TO EXHAUSTION

MIXED SIGNALS

HILLARY IS A STRONG CANDIDATE WHO CAN *EASILY* BEAT TRUMP--

--IF SHE HASN'T BEEN IRREVOCABLY *DAMAGED* BY *BERNIE SANDERS!*

A SIMPLE PLAN

WE JUST HAVE TO HIGHLIGHT TRUMP'S MANY INTEMPERATE *REMARKS*-- AND WE'LL WIN IN A *LANDSLIDE!*

BRILLIANT! VOTERS PROBABLY HAVEN'T *HEARD* ABOUT THAT SIDE OF HIM YET!

LIFE DURING WARTIME

THAT *THING* THAT JUST HAPPENED DISCREDITS *YOUR* CANDIDATE'S ENTIRE *CAMPAIGN!*

THE THING THAT HAPPENED AFTER *THAT* PROVES *YOUR* CANDIDATE IS THE *WORST HUMAN WHO EVER LIVED!*

BLISS OF THE PUNDITOCRACY

WHO'S *UP*? WHO'S *DOWN*? WHAT'S *NEXT*?

WE'LL BE CHITTER-CHATTERING AUTHORITATIVELY FOR THE NEXT SIX *MONTHS!*

BEATS THE HELL OUT OF *WORKING!*

THE NUMBERS GAME

THE DATA IS UTTERLY CONCLUSIVE-- TRUMP CANNOT *POSSIBLY* WIN!

BROAD SWATHS OF THE ELECTORATE WOULD HAVE TO BE *SEETHING* WITH RACISM AND MISOGYNY!

BUT WHAT ARE THE ODDS OF *THAT*?

HOPE BURNS ETERNAL

IF WE BUILD A *TIME MACHINE* AND KEEP THE SUPERDELEGATES FROM EVER BEING *BORN*--

--THEN *BERNIE* STILL HAS A PATH TO *VICTORY!*

THE QUEST FOR UNITY

OKAY, SURE, WE SAID BERNIE VOTERS WERE SCUM-SUCKING *VERMIN* BENT ON THE DESTRUCTION OF ALL THAT IS GOOD AND DECENT--

--BUT WE MEANT IT IN THE NICEST POSSIBLE *WAY!*

NEXT: THE DEATH OF SATIRE

STUPID CARTOONISTS! YOU THINK *YOU* CAN COME UP WITH JOKES THAT ARE MORE ABSURD THAN *MY ACTUAL BEHAVIOR*?

HA HA! SAD!

TOM TOMORROW ©2016

126

THIS MODERN WORLD

by TOM TOMORROW

DONALD TRUMP IS GOING TO MAKE AMERICA **GREAT** AGAIN!

YES, AS THE HAT PROCLAIMS. BUT WHEN WAS THAT, EXACTLY?

WHAT?

TO WHICH GOLDEN ERA OF THE PAST, EXACTLY, WILL PRESIDENT TRUMP RETURN US?

ER--I--

HE'S NEVER SPECIFIED--ACCORDING TO A SURVEY RELEASED A FEW WEEKS AGO, THE YEAR MOST FREQUENTLY CHOSEN BY YOUR FELLOW TRUMP **SUPPORTERS** WAS 2000.*

WORKS FOR ME! BACK BEFORE OBAMACARE AND ALL THIS **TERRORISM!**

*TRUE!

SO YOU'RE SAYING AMERICA WAS GREAT IMMEDIATELY BEFORE THE START OF THE LAST REPUBLICAN ADMINISTRATION? YOU'D LIKE TO HIT THE RESET BUTTON AND TAKE US BACK TO THE TAIL END OF THE **CLINTON** YEARS?

DONALD TRUMP WILL MAKE AMERICA GREAT AGAIN--LIKE NEVER **BEFORE!**

IS THERE A WORD TO DESCRIBE THE SENSATION OF GREAT AMUSEMENT MIXED WITH SHEER DREAD?

I DUNNO. WHY?

JUST SEEMS LIKE IT MIGHT COME IN HANDY.

TOM TOMORROW © 2016

DONALD TRUMP SAYS/DOES/TWEETS **ANOTHER** INCOMPREHENSIBLY AWFUL THING.

HEH HEH! TAKE **THAT**, CROOKED HILLARY!

THIS IS **EXTREMELY** PRESIDENTIAL BEHAVIOR-- THE **BEST!** THAT I CAN TELL YOU.

START HERE!

AND **THEN**--

AND THEN--

HIS SUPPORTERS DOUBLE DOWN.

THE LYING MEDIA ARE LYING **AGAIN!** MISTER TRUMP **NEVER** SAID/DID/ TWEETED THE INCOMPREHENSIBLY AWFUL THING!

UNLESS HE **DID,** IN WHICH CASE IT WAS AN **AWESOME** THING TO SAY/DO/TWEET!

THE CYCLE OF TRUMP
ROUND AND ROUND AND ROUND IT GOES

SANE PEOPLE REACT WITH DISBELIEF.

DID YOU SEE THE **LATEST** INCOMPREHENSIBLY AWFUL THING HE DID/SAID/TWEETED?

SURELY HE HAS GONE TOO FAR **THIS** TIME!

JOURNALISTS TRY TO KEEP UP.

--AND THE MOST RECENT TRUMP CONTROVERSY CONTINUES TO **GROW!**

WE **MIGHT** GET TO THE END OF THE HOUR BEFORE HE SAYS/ DOES/TWEETS SOMETHING EVEN **MORE** INCOMPREHENSIBLY AWFUL!

AND THEN--

AND THEN--

TOM TOMORROW ©2016

128

THIS MODERN WORLD

by TOM TOMORROW

IT'S TIME AGAIN FOR GUN TALK WITH YOUR HOST, THE GLIB SOCIOPATH

THANKS FOR SUBSCRIBING TO MY CHANNEL! OUR TOPIC TODAY IS THE LATEST REGRETTABLE MASS MORTALITY INCIDENT IN WHICH FIREARMS *HAPPENED* TO PLAY A ROLE!

IT GOES WITHOUT SAYING THAT WE IN THE FIREARM-AMERICAN COMMUNITY *DEPLORE* THESE MYSTERIOUS, ENTIRELY UNPREVENTABLE TRAGEDIES!

BUT THERE'S NO POINT IN IGNORANTLY SCAPEGOATING INNOCENT *GUNS*!

MOST GUN GRABBERS DON'T EVEN UNDERSTAND THE DIFFERENCE BETWEEN THE DIRECT IMPINGEMENT SYSTEM OF AN *AR-15* AND THE GAS PISTON OPERATION OF A *SIG SAUER MCX*!

HA HA! THEY'RE NOT QUALIFIED TO EVEN *HAVE* OPINIONS ABOUT GUN CONTROL!

OF COURSE, WE MUSTN'T *POLITICIZE* THE ISSUE! THE ONLY *APPROPRIATE* RESPONSE AT A MOMENT LIKE THIS IS TO TWEET SINCERE-SOUNDING *CONDOLENCES*!

@AmericanGunLuvver4EVER
Thoughts and prayers to the victims who were killed by firearms but could just as easily have drowned in swimming pools!

TAP TAP TAP

BUT WE MUST BE *REALISTIC*! OCCASIONAL, REGRETTABLE MASS MORTALITY INCIDENTS ARE JUST THE PRICE AMERICANS *PAY*--

--FOR OUR SECOND-HALF-OF-THE-SECOND-AMENDMENT *RIGHT* TO PURCHASE THE *REALLY BITCHIN'* MILITARY GRADE WEAPONS OF OUR *CHOICE*!

FOR SELF DEFENSE AND STUFF.

NOW LET'S TALK ABOUT BANNING ALL MUSLIMS AND BUILDING A GIANT WALL ALONG THE ENTIRE MEXICAN BORDER.

YOU KNOW-- *PRACTICAL* SOLUTIONS!

SOON, AND FOR THE REST OF YOUR LIFE: MORE OF THE *SAME*!

TOM TOMORROW ©2016

THIS MODERN WORLD

by TOM TOMORROW

THIS IS ALL VERY, VERY NORMAL

TWELVE MONTHS OF TRUMP (AND COUNTING)

A PERFECTLY ORDINARY CAMPAIGN ROLLOUT.

"(MEXICANS) ARE BRINGING DRUGS...CRIME...THEY'RE **RAPISTS**..."

"...AND SOME, I ASSUME, ARE GOOD PEOPLE."

STATESMANLIKE REMARKS ON JOHN McCAIN--

"**HE'S** NOT A WAR HERO... I LIKE PEOPLE WHO **WEREN'T** CAPTURED!"

--AND MEGYN KELLY.

"THERE WAS BLOOD COMING OUT OF HER EYES, BLOOD COMING OUT OF HER **WHEREVER!**"

THAT TIME SOMEONE ASKED "WHEN CAN WE GET RID OF" MUSLIMS.

"WE'RE GOING TO BE LOOKING AT A **LOT** OF DIFFERENT THINGS!"

MOCKING A REPORTER'S DISABILITY.

"YOU GOTTA SEE THIS GUY!"

"AUUGH! ARRGH!"

RIDICULING AN ENTIRE STATE.

"HOW STUPID **ARE** THE PEOPLE OF IOWA?"

BEARING FALSE WITNESS.

"I WATCHED WHEN THE WORLD TRADE CENTER CAME TUMBLING DOWN... AND I WATCHED IN JERSEY CITY, WHERE THOUSANDS OF PEOPLE WERE **CHEERING!**"

BLACKLISTING NUMEROUS MAJOR MEDIA OUTLETS FROM HIS EVENTS, THOUGH HELPFULLY CLARIFYING--

"I HATE SOME OF THESE (REPORTERS)--BUT I'D NEVER **KILL** THEM!"

STANDING UP FOR TORTURE.

"IF IT DOESN'T WORK, THEY DESERVE IT ANYWAY, FOR WHAT THEY ARE DOING!"

THAT DOCTOR'S NOTE.

"If elected, Mr. Trump, I can state unequivocally, will be the healthiest individual ever elected to the presidency."

THE **USA FREEDOM KIDS!**

"DEAL FROM STRENGTH, OR GET CRUSHED EVERY **TIME!**"

THE VERY SCARY REPORTER.

"SHE HAD A **PEN** IN HER HAND, (MAYBE) IT'S A LITTLE **BOMB!**"

THE PROPOSAL TO BAN ALL MUSLIMS--

"--UNTIL WE FIGURE OUT WHAT'S GOING **ON!**"

EXTREMELY PRESIDENTIAL REACTIONS TO PROTESTERS.

"I'D LIKE TO PUNCH (THEM) IN THE **FACE!**"

DEFENDING HIS PENIS ON NATIONAL TV.

"I GUARANTEE YOU THERE'S NO PROBLEM. I **GUARANTEE.**"

PUZZLED BY INCOMPREHENSIBLE QUESTIONS.

"I DON'T KNOW **ANYTHING** ABOUT...WHITE SUPREMACY... I KNOW **NOTHING** ABOUT DAVID DUKE!"

ENTIRELY RATIONAL QUESTIONS ABOUT TED CRUZ'S FATHER.

"WHAT WAS HE **DOING** WITH LEE HARVEY OSWALD SHORTLY BEFORE THE DEATH, BEFORE THE SHOOTING? IT'S **HORRIBLE!**"

VEHEMENTLY DENYING THAT HE POSES AS OWN PUBLICIST.

"IT WAS NOT **ME** ON THE PHONE!"

(ADMITTED IN 1990 COURT HEARING THAT HE POSES AS OWN PUBLICIST.)

THAT CINCO DE MAYO TWEET.

"The best taco bowls are made in Trump Tower Grill. I love Hispanics!"

EXPLAINING WHY A JUDGE BORN IN INDIANA SHOULD RECUSE HIMSELF IN A LAWSUIT AGAINST TRUMP.

"HE'S A **MEXICAN!**"

"WE'RE BUILDING A **WALL!**"

REPEATEDLY INSISTING, AS ONE DOES--

"--I AM THE LEAST RACIST PERSON YOU'VE EVER **ENCOUNTERED!**"

(SEE ALSO: FREQUENT RETWEETING OF WHITE SUPREMACISTS.)

TWEETING "CONGRATS" TO SELF FOR "BEING RIGHT" AFTER ORLANDO MASSACRE; INSINUATING THAT OBAMA SECRETLY SUPPORTS ISIS.

"(HE IS) EITHER NOT TOUGH, NOT SMART--"

"--OR HE'S GOT SOMETHING **ELSE** IN MIND!"

NOTING THAT BREXIT ECONOMIC TURMOIL WILL BENEFIT HIS SCOTTISH GOLF COURSE.

"WHEN THE POUND GOES DOWN--"

"--MORE PEOPLE ARE COMING TO **TURNBERRY**, FRANKLY!"

MAKE AMERICA GREAT AGAIN

NEXT: **MORE** TOTALLY NORMAL BEHAVIOR!

"I'VE **ALWAYS** HEARD PEOPLE SAY--DONALD, YOU HAVE THE MOST **BEAUTIFUL HANDS!**"

"SLIGHTLY **LARGE**, ACTUALLY!"

THIS MODERN WORLD

by TOM TOMORROW

DOCTOR WHO VS. THE BREXIT

HELLO, I'M THE *DOCTOR*! I'M A *TIME LORD* FROM THE PLANET *GALLIFREY*!

SO YOU'RE AN *ALIEN*, THEN?

WELL, TECHNICALLY-- BUT I *VISIT* THE U.K. *OFTEN*!

YOU SEE, MY *TARDIS* ALLOWS ME TO TRAVEL *ANYWHERE* IN ALL OF SPACE AND TIME! COME ON--YOU WANT TO GO FOR A SPIN?

I SHOULD CERTAINLY THINK *NOT*!

BUT-- *WHY*?

THE *PAST* IS OBVIOUSLY FULL OF *TEEMING MASSES*--AND THE *FUTURE* IS UNDOUBTEDLY OVERRUN WITH ALIEN *BUREAUCRATS* TELLING EVERYONE WHAT TO *DO*!

WELL--WE *DO* HAVE THE *SHADOW PROCLAMATION*--

AND THE BRITISH PEOPLE WANT NO *PART* OF IT! WHATEVER IT IS.

WAIT--WHO *ARE* YOU TWO, ANY- WAY?

HAH! YOU FOOL--*WE* ARE POLITICIANS WHO JUST WHIPPED UP A NATIONALISTIC *FRENZY*, TO PERSUADE BRITISH VOTERS TO LEAVE THE EUROPEAN UNION--

--ECONOMIC CONSEQUENCES BE *DAMNED*!

RIGHT! SO THIS MUST BE THE PART--

--WHERE YOU TURN OUT TO BE HORRIBLE MONSTERS IN HUMAN DISGUISE, SCHEMING TO SPREAD *CHAOS* AND *DISCORD* AMONGST THE UNSUSPECTING POPULATION! GO ON THEN--TAKE THE COSTUMES *OFF*!

SORRY, DOCTOR--WE AL- *READY* REVEALED OUR TRUE NATURES--

--AND WE WON *ANYWAY*!

NEXT: AN UNEXPECTED *TWIST*!

ALL RIGHT THEN, LADS--CARRY ON! *MY* WORK HERE IS DONE!

EXCUSE ME?

?

AND *THEN*... BUT--BUT--I'M A BELOVED BRITISH *ICON*!

EH--TELL IT TO THE *DEPORTATION TRIBUNAL*!

TOM TOMORROW ©2016...APOLOGIES TO THE BBC AND PETER CAPALDI!

THIS MODERN WORLD

by TOM TOMORROW

Panel 1:

HELLO, PROFESSOR! WHAT ARE YOU WORKING ON **NOW**?

WELL, BILLY--YOU MAY HAVE NOTICED THAT THERE'S A LOT OF **TURMOIL** IN THE WORLD LATELY...

Panel 2:

TERRORISM, ENDLESS WARS, MASS SHOOTINGS, GLOBAL WARMING, RISING NATIONALISM, THE BREXIT, ECONOMIC UNCERTAINTY, POLICE KILLING CIVILIANS, LUNATICS KILLING POLICE--

--AND A NOT-INSIGNIFICANT NUMBER OF AMERICANS READY TO VOTE FOR **DONALD TRUMP** IN NOVEMBER.

Panel 3:

HOWEVER--ACCORDING TO MY COMPUTATIONS, NONE OF THIS IS **REALLY** HAPPENING! RATHER, WE ARE **CHARACTERS** IN SOME SORT OF HEAVY-HANDED **POLITICAL SATIRE** CREATED BY AN AUTHOR ON A HIGHER PLANE OF EXISTENCE-- THE "REAL WORLD," IF YOU WILL.

Panel 4:

CONSIDER: IF THESE EVENTS WERE **GENUINE**, THE ONLY CONCLUSION WOULD BE THAT WE ARE TOO STUPID AS A SPECIES TO **SURVIVE**! WHY WOULD WE REFUSE TO ADDRESS UNDERLYING PROBLEMS LIKE RACISM, OR GUNS, OR CLIMATE CHANGE?

AND MOST DECISIVELY, WHY WOULD **ANYONE** CONSIDER DONALD TRUMP QUALIFIED FOR THE PRESIDENCY?

Panel 5:

CLEARLY, WE ARE LIVING IN A HAMFISTED SATIRICAL NOVEL--OR PERHAPS A **CARTOON**, IF ANYONE READS **THOSE** ANYMORE.

UNFORTUNATELY, WE ARE AT THE MERCY OF AN AUTHOR WHO HAS REPEATEDLY SHOWN COMPLETE DISREGARD FOR ANY **SEMBLANCE** OF LOGIC OR RATIONALITY--

Panel 6:

--AS WELL AS A PROPENSITY FOR POINTLESS NIHILISM AND OVER-THE-TOP PLOT TWISTS.

UH--PROFESSOR--?

TOM TOMORROW ©2016

THIS MODERN WORLD

by TOM TOMORROW

photo credit: J.P. Trostle

Tom Tomorrow is the nom de cartoon used by Dan Perkins, creator of the weekly political strip *This Modern World*. His work appears online at sites including *Daily Kos* and *The Nation*, and has been a mainstay of alternative papers across the country for 25 years. His cartoons and illustrations have been featured in the *New York Times, the New Yorker, The American Prospect, The Economist, Esquire, Forbes, In These Times, Mother Jones, Newsweek, Spin, TV Guide, U.S. News & World Report,* and many other fine publications. Kurt Vonnegut once called him "[T]he wry voice of American common sense, humor, and decency which has been scorned or ignored by big-time journalists."

He was the 2013 recipient of the Herblock Prize, and was awarded the first place Robert F. Kennedy Journalism Award for Cartooning on two occasions, in 1998 and again in 2003. He was a finalist for the Pulitzer Prize in 2015, and has received numerous other honors, including the first place Association of Alternative Newsweeklies Award for Cartooning and the James Aronson Award for Social Justice Journalism.

In 2009, he collaborated with the band Pearl Jam to create the artwork for their album *Backspacer*.

He is the author of ten previous cartoon anthologies and one book for children. In July 2015 he raised $310,537 from 3,098 Kickstarter backers to finance the publication of a two-volume, thousand-page hardcover career retrospective, *25 Years of Tomorrow*.

Dan Perkins lives outside of New Haven, Connecticut, with his wife and son.